WHY ME?

"For every tear you've cried, for every pain you've endured, God has a plan and it's good!"

Beverly D. Thomas is an amazing and inspirational woman of God. Through the unction and power of the Holy Spirit, she has masterfully produced a delightful combination of scriptures and real-life applications to be used as a spiritual roadmap for living a Christ-centered life. Congratulations to Beverly for offering such a powerful and much needed personal and practical guide that deals with the core of spiritual issues in every Christian believer's life. *Why Me?* is a priceless collection of powerful biblical examples that will move you to look at your life anew. If you have any desire to find the life God offers you, read this book.

—Rev. Larry E. Campbell, MDiv
Pastor, St. Paul A.M.E. Church

This work is an extraordinary accomplishment! It is a sincere and honest portrayal of personal stories, inspirational experiences, and biblical exhortations that can serve as one's daily devotional.

—Dr. D.C. Nosakhere Thomas
Senior Apostle
Rainbow Community Praise Center International

Beverly D. Thomas is a loving Christian woman who's writing mirrors her life. This book, written in obedience to His will, is truly inspired by God. It is a must read!

—Cheryl Brown
Award-Winning Publisher And Entrepreneur

Beverly D. Thomas is a child of God who has been graced with a love and affection for all. While her book is entitled *Why Me?*, I answer, "Why not you?" I see in Beverly the qualities of faithfulness. Her willingness of spirit allows her to share with her readers this wonderful testimony of encouragement; blessing them while planting seeds of hope. *Why Me?* will truly uplift and enlighten all who read it.

—Dr. Margaret B. Hill
Educator, Philanthropist & Author

After reading this spirit filled manuscript *Why Me?*, it is clear that the author sets out to explore the genuine nature of man and the essential principles for walking, living, and operating in the spiritual realm. The subject matter reaches down into the core elements of how to experience a mature Christian life. Beverly Thomas is not afraid to deal with the major issues facing marriage, single life, and leadership in and outside the church.

Beverly has poured her heart and talents into this work in an effort to refocus and re-energize our God-given assignment of being a change agent in a world that is in great need. Moreover, the book inspires those willing to assess where they are; causing them to inquire "why me?" This book teaches that our God-given purpose impacts others and our community for the better, removing all excuses for not moving forward. We are blessed to be a blessing to others; we are lights in a dark place; and we are called to help others. *Why Me?* reminds us to strive toward being the spiritual person that God originally desired for us.

—Dr. Ernest B. Dowdy, Bishop
Church of the Living God

I recommend *Why Me?* as a must-read for every believer. Beverly has revealed God's process to healing, freedom, and wholeness found in Scripture. After reading this book, you will be equipped with the right mind set needed to overcome addictive habits and cycles of self-destruction that hinder us from experiencing the joy, peace, and purpose that God has for all of us.

—Pastor Marco Garcia
The Way World Outreach Ministries

WHY ME?

"For every tear you've cried, for every pain you've
endured, God has a plan and it's good!"

BEVERLY D. THOMAS

**CREATION
HOUSE**

WHY ME? by Beverly D. Thomas
Published by Creation House
A Charisma Media Company
600 Rinehart Road
Lake Mary, Florida 32746
www.charismamedia.com

All Scripture quotations are from the King James Version of the Bible.

Definitions are from *Merriam-Webster's Collegiate Dictionary Eleventh Edition* (Springfield, MA: Merriam-Webster, 2003).

Design Director: Bill Johnson
Cover design by Nancy Panaccione

Visit the author's website: Beverlythomas.com

Library of Congress Cataloging-in-Publication Data: 2011942171
International Standard Book Number: 978-1-61638-824-9
E-book International Standard Book Number: 978-1-61638-825-6

While the author has made every effort to provide accurate telephone numbers and Internet addresses at the time of publication, neither the publisher nor the author assumes any responsibility for errors or for changes that occur after publication.

First edition

11 12 13 14 15 — 987654321
Printed in Canada

DEDICATION

This book is lovingly dedicated to the memory of my mother Donna M. Bailey, my grandmother Reba Williams, and my sister Flora Jean Beard. To my three children, Casie, Cortney, and Tyler, and my three grandchildren, Tyler, Faith, and Jordan. Thank you for walking through these lessons of love with me. I love you.

ACKNOWLEDGMENTS

To my Lord and Savior Jesus Christ who has truly been my rock, my fortress, my strong tower, and the lover of my soul, I simply say Thank you! There are many individuals, too many to name, who have had a profound impact on my life and to whom I credit the tenacity it took for me to obey the mandate of God to publish this book. Of greatest importance are my beautiful children: Casie, Cortney, and Tyler, and my precious grandchildren, Tyler, Faith, and Jordan…you gave me reason to go on when I had none. Thank you for your patience, your endurance, and your unwavering love for me. You have taught me so much and it seems as if we've switched roles and I am the one who's learning from you. You continue to be a blessing in my life in ways you will never know.

- To Barrion, my ex-husband and my best friend, your unwavering support and encouragement are immeasurable. I love you still!

- To one of the most beautiful women I know, my sister Clarice Henry, you are a shining example of true grace. At my weakest point, you encouraged me with your words of wisdom and gave me strength to go to the next level. Thank you!

- To mama Geri, a true Proverbs 31 woman, you open your mouth with wisdom and in your tongue is the law of kindness. Thank you for gracing my life. I love you!

- To my adoptive moms, Margaret B. Hill and Cheryl Brown, you are shining examples of virtuous women. Your unconditional love and acceptance is a powerful force that carries with it the ability to catapult simplicity into greatness. I want to be just like you both when I grow up!

- To my wonderful friend and mentor, Pastor Larry E. Campbell, St. Paul AME, San Bernardino, California, thank you for preaching the uncompromising Word of God and being a living epistle of the Word you preach. Your passion and love for Christ is revealed in the childlike excitement that you exhibit when you speak of Him. As you speak, you cease and the Christ in you is unveiled; it is a wonderful sight! I am blessed to share time and space with you my friend.

- Dr. D.C. Nosakhere Thomas, Pastor, Rainbow Community Praise Center, Fontana, California; thank you for the many years of encouragement, guidance and support. Your uncompromising preaching of the gospel and your life of integrity, make you a rare gift to all who are blessed to encounter you.

- To my Pastor, Marco Garcia, at The Way World Outreach Church, San Bernardino, California. Thank you for obeying the call and mandate of God to reach out to the hurting and broken. One only need attend a Sunday service to witness the power of God in operation.

- Last, but definitely not least, Dr. Ernest B. Dowdy, Jr.; presiding Bishop, a visionary whose sees through the eyes of his heart. You see what others miss. Thank you for gracing my life.

I love you all!

CONTENTS

PREFACE

THE BIBLE IS a storybook. The characters are real, and the events are true. This Book was so powerful in God's mind that He decided to create a real-life portrayal of it. We are living or portraying the words of God, which were spoken into existence before the world began. The characters in the book are people who have lived before us; their experiences are an example to guide us. The end has already been set. Like an actor, our job is to read the script and portray our part in this great historical movie. In order to understand our purpose, the purpose of God through us, we must read the script. We must follow every line under the direction and leadership of the Director, God.

This book is a series of divine insights into the mind, the heart, and the will of God for man. In order to understand, to comprehend, to make sense of the now and prepare for the future, we must understand the past. From the fall of Adam and Eve to the return of Jesus, God's sole purpose for humanity has been to reconcile us back to Him, to give us life, and that more abundantly. God, our Father, desires the best for us.

Go with me as we take a journey into the past, the future, and finally, the present as we explore the heart of God, the mind of Christ, and the purpose of the Holy Spirit for humanity. As we delve into the spirit realm, the revelations will overwhelm you. They will inspire you to be all that God has intended for you to be. You will be propelled into an atmosphere of love, kindness, and joy unspeakable, and one full of glory, victory, and liberty.

As you read the inspired Word of God, allow God to speak to you, to answer those questions you have, and reveal the mystery of His love to you. I pray that the transforming power of the Holy Spirit will fill your soul and transform your mind as you read each page.

As you reach each chapter, I believe that by the power of the Holy Spirit the garments of bondage will begin to unravel. By the end of the book you will not only be set free, but you will most assuredly know *why you!*

INTRODUCTION

I T SEEMS SELFISH to put the emphasis on the me, but without allowing Christ to transform the me, there are no theys. As Christians, we believe that it is our purpose, our duty, to be born again, grow up and mature, and become useful for someone else. We feel that the emphasis on our own self, our own problems, our own families and responsibilities in some way hinders us from accomplishing the will of God as interpreted by us from the Scriptures, which is to preach the gospel. We then "go forth," or go into ministry (the thing that God has called us to), and we leave the rest for God to handle. In the old cliché "If we take care of God's business, God will take care of ours" we miss the fact that "in the beginning" God created man in His image with specific instructions and later gave man a helpmeet, a wife, along with instructions to subdue the earth, to be fruitful, and to multiply.

IN THE BEGINNING

From the beginning it was God's intention for man to reproduce after himself and for every other creature to reproduce after his or her own kind. If we are broken, hurt, insecure, then that is what we will reproduce. The Bible asks the question, How can we get the mote out of someone else's eye when there is a beam in our own? (See Luke 6:42.) Christians hear a word from God, we feel that we are called, and we spend the next several years trying to convince everyone else of this

1

fact. The reality, however, is that there is no fruit being produced by this tree we claim to be. Why?

THE PROCESS

The portions of Scripture we somehow ignore are the ones dealing with the process of the lives of the men and women spoken of in the Bible. It is important to remember that before ministry, many of these men and women had somewhat disastrous lives. They were sinners in the worst way. In order for God to completely regenerate us, we must not just know in theory, know in our mind, but we must be repulsed by the reality that our best is as filthy rags in God's sight. We must understand that if we reproduce in an unhealthy state, we will reproduce unhealthy offspring. If a drug-addicted mother gives birth to a baby, the baby is born drug exposed. This means that there are drugs in the baby's system, and reactions such as continuous crying, loss of appetite, jitters, and low birth weight are all initial signs of the exposure. However, if this mother had been healthy and conscious of the health of her unborn child during pregnancy, then chances are great that the unborn child would have been a healthy one. Knowing this, it should be our heart's desire and we should be driven by the knowledge, the need, and the necessity for God to regenerate us before He allows our lives to reproduce.

Often victims of abuse (physical, mental, or sexual) grow up and have children without having ever dealt either in the natural or in the spirit with the profound effects of this abuse. When they have children, they more often than not exercise the same abuse on their children. Reproduction without regeneration is a recipe for disaster.

It is not in our ability to understand the infinite wisdom

of God. The wisest man in the world, King Solomon, concluded that life was all foolishness. The only reality, the only truth, the only thing worth knowing is that God is God. Life in the flesh had meaning before the fall of man, when man had an understanding of God. However, through sin, the evil that was never to touch man's heart entered in as a seed, took root, and grew into an enormous source of power. This evil brought forth such a gap between God and man that man was unable to understand or comprehend the mind of God. Jesus's whole ministry was an act of showing us and teaching us through our sinful minds and limited understanding the mind of God. Jesus did not speak in parables simply because it was an easy way to learn, nor because He thought it was cute. He spoke in parables because the natural mind was incapable of understanding spiritual things. He spoke of spiritual things in the natural sense for our natural understanding. Jesus said that after the Holy Ghost comes *He* would bring those things back to your remembrance. The Holy Ghost is the One who causes those natural parables of Jesus to become spiritual food to us. The Holy Spirit makes the spiritual things understandable to us.

REGENERATION

The regeneration process is so excruciatingly painful to us that with everything that is within it, the flesh will attempt to dismiss the whole process. We take the portion of the process that we feel we need. You see, we are the ones in control. We have the Holy Spirit, the wisdom of God, and we know what portion of the regeneration process should apply to us. We are not going though "that particular process" because we don't need that one. Having a sinful nature, we know that our flesh is enmity against God; still, through pride and rebellion we decide what portion of us God needs to fix. God said that He "gave them over to a reprobate mind" (Rom. 1:28). Simply stated, God said, "You don't need me. I'll pull back." God does not need to send a curse. He does not need to give the devil permission to attack; man's own sinful nature and desire will destroy the reprobate man.

You see, we give the devil too much credit. While we are blaming the devil for the attacks against us, Satan is sitting back with his arms crossed in complete arrogance in the knowing that he is so tough that he commands obedience to himself without lifting a finger. God has to show His unconditional love toward us in order for us to be drawn wholeheartedly to Him. On the other hand, Satan does not have to do anything, and we bow to him in complete service. Man wills destruction unto himself. He absolutely desires destruction. Therefore, man's desire must change—not an easy task.

If I, having been regenerated through Christ in the spirit, have not yet experienced the full manifestation of this in the natural, then it stands to reason that God still has much work yet to be done in me. If my whole mind, body, and spirit are not yet in total submission to the will of God, the voice of the Holy Spirit; if I have not yet fully comprehended that Jesus Christ is my everything, past, present, and future, and that His character must replace mine in all areas, then I am not yet ready for His ministry.

Is this way of thinking selfish? There is an old spiritual that says, "It's me, it's me, it's me, oh Lord, standing in the need of prayer." Paul states, "O wretched man that I am! who shall deliver me from this...?" (Rom. 7:24). Job states, "I abhor myself" (Job 42:6). David cried out for God to purge him with hyssop, and Moses told the Lord he was a man of limited speech. The greatest confession of all came from the apostle Paul, who called himself a chief sinner (1 Tim. 1:15).

Paul stated that he did not consult with man but that he went away to Assyria into the desert for three years so that God could deal with him before he ever even heard the gospel preached, ever laid eyes on an apostle, or even attempted to preach the gospel.

In every story, from the account of the lives of the prophets of old to the account of the lives of the apostles, none went forth into ministry until God had completed the work of regeneration in him. It stands to reason, what could a man not completely regenerated have to tell me? Before the conversation is over, it will be about the man, not Jesus. Jesus spoke only of the Father, His will, His purpose, and His plan for the people. Jesus said that His food was to do the will of the Father. (See John 4:34.) Jesus had no plans, no opinions, no ideas, and no struggles. The purpose of God was yea and amen. Naturally, Jesus would not accomplish God's great work without obstacles.

God's Timing

One must remember that Jesus did not enter ministry until He was thirty years old, and seek to understand why. There are a lot of men and women in our present time who do not enter into ministry until that time or even later, but what sets Jesus apart is that before His time of entrance He was already enormously wise, very intelligent, and well-versed in Scripture. Although tempted in every area as we are, He was totally and completely without sin. Jesus had not the burden of a wife or children, and He worked in the family business. Jesus grew up in a Christian home and likely never heard a curse word or any idle word spoken in His house. In addition to being God Incarnate, He did not have the dysfunction in His home, as many of us did. Sure, He had to endure the gossip about His mother having a virgin birth and His claim of being the Messiah, but the teasing was not much different than what children today experience. In addition, He had divine impartation and knowledge, having been born of God.

Jesus understood that the spiritual law was limited by the natural law of the flesh, and He, even being the Son of God, had to deal with the issues of the flesh. It took the Son of God thirty years to deal with the flesh. Who do we think we are? The Scriptures tell us that at one point at age twelve, Jesus went into the temple to preach, and the Christian leaders were amazed at His wisdom. But soon mom came, and in a language that would be equivalent to our words today, she told Him to get Himself home. Mary, by the wisdom of God, knew that this child was not to exceed God's timing. I am sure that she looked at her son in amazement because of His great wisdom, but being chosen by God to bear this child, she was given wisdom as to His upbringing. Jesus was not to go forth into ministry before God's appointed time, and His parents made sure of it.

God has given His people elders and bishops to guide and direct us. These are men and women who have already gone through the process and have now been called to go forth into ministry. Like Joseph and Mary, God has given these anointed men and women divine insight into the people they shepherd. If there has been no shepherd, if there has been no blessing, no proper dismissal, then chances are it is not time.

Peter sent forth Barnabas, Stephen, and many other great men of God into ministry. The apostle Paul commissioned men to start churches in different areas. These men themselves went through the process of regeneration. These are those who not only rejected God in some way or another, but they had their filth revealed to them. They saw the raw of themselves, the depth of the evil within them, and desired that Jesus would completely regenerate them. They were not satisfied with a knowing of Christ; they wanted to be transformed into His image and likeness. It was after their own transformation that they became eligible, or worthy, to be a partaker of Christ's suffering. You see, we talk about reigning with Christ, being a victor with Christ, being a joint heir with Christ, but we really go around that "suffering with Christ" part. We skirt over the "take up your cross" portion of this reality.

Is it selfish to continuously have thoughts about me, how unworthy I am, to continuously ask God to heal me, to purge me? As long as I do, I can be sure that God is still showing me, me, and the humility that comes through this knowing can only be imparted by the Holy Spirit. A prideful man no longer sees himself unworthy; he sees himself done. Only a man striving to be one with Christ will seek to have the me continuously regenerated. It is not at a point that the regeneration process in us is done that Christ uses us. It is at a point of complete and total, unwavering understanding of our need for Him that He can use us. Until we can look into a mirror and see Christ quickened in our mortal bodies, it is an absolute must that me is at the forefront of our prayer for them.

Chapter 1

THE WORD MADE OF FLESH

In the beginning was the Word, and the Word was with God, and the Word was God. The same was in the beginning with God.

—JOHN 1:1–2

H
E WHO WAS come is come, and He who is come did come! What was to happen has happened, and what is to happen did happen!

God told a story, the story was documented in heaven, and it was good. God decided to give life to this story. He spoke to the story and caused every part of it to come alive, except the human portion. This portion was to be God's greatest, most personal masterpiece. This He would do with His own hands. God, along with His Son, decided to make this human, or "man," in His own image. He formed man and saw that he was fearfully and wonderfully made. However, man had no life, no soul, and no spirit. Man needed God's Spirit to come alive, and he needed a soul (a mind and will) so that he would freely love his Creator. But God wanted more; He wanted offspring. He knew that this man Adam could not produce offspring of his own, so he created a woman for him, blessed them, and told them to be fruitful and multiply and replenish the earth.

Since God wrote the story, He of course knew the end. God knew that man would use this freedom of will to become independent of God. So, then, why would God not just create

9

a people who would always obey him? God is love. God's existence is love, His character is love, and God wanted His human creation to freely love Him because of His majesty and not out of force. God knew that His unwavering love toward this sinful people would eventually cause them to willfully appreciate and love Him back. He knew that the sacrifice of His Son on behalf of the people would prove His love for them and would cause them to love Him in return.

In the Book of Isaiah, God told His Son:

> He shall see of the travail of his soul, and shall be satisfied: by his knowledge shall my righteous servant justify many; for he shall bear their iniquities.
>
> —ISAIAH 53:11

You see, from the beginning God has desired our love, so much so that He sacrificed His Son to prove His love for us.

THE FALL

Beginning from the fall of Adam and Eve until the death, burial, and resurrection of Jesus, man wandered about in a fog. Except for the prophets, who were led by God in wisdom for His people, the people had no direction, and their knowledge of God was that which was revealed to them by these prophets. Man was unable to have direct communion with God because sin had separated us from God. As we know, God cannot look upon sin, and there had been no redemption made for our sin. Although the people had breath in their bodies, they were as "walking dead." Their bodies and minds were increasingly deteriorating, and the sin was increasing in magnitude.

God had a plan of redemption that would require human cooperation. The man who became the father of nations would produce a seed that against all odds would bring forth the Messiah. This great man, Abraham, and his son Isaac would be a shadow of God and Christ. While Abraham would be called to sacrifice his only begotten son, his promised seed, God would ultimately spare Isaac and instead use Abraham's seed to bring forth His own Son. Abraham's act of obedience served as a metaphor for the ultimate sacrifice, Jesus Christ. It was through Abraham's obedience that God, in Genesis 22:13, provided a ram for Abraham to sacrifice unto God, and it was there that God spoke to Abraham and told him that "in thy seed shall all the nations of the earth be blessed; because thou hast obeyed my voice" (Gen. 22:18).

THE PLAN OF REDEMPTION

"God so loved the world, that he gave his only begotten Son, that whosoever believeth in him should not perish, but have everlasting life" (John 3:16). It is important to understand that Jesus did not become God's Son after He was manifested in the earth; He was with God in heaven from the beginning. Jesus had a Father-and-Son relationship with the Creator before the world began, yet He was asked to come and live in a dry, evil world, suffer, and then die so that man might be redeemed through Him.

The Bible gives us some insight into the conversation that this Father and Son had, and after being told of the things that He would have to suffer, Jesus pleaded with the Father that this cup would pass from Him. Isaiah 50:5–6 speaks of Jesus's obedience to God. Jesus speaks about how He gave His back to the whip and His cheeks to those who pulled out His beard. He speaks of the shame and how He did not hide from it, and He mentions that they spit in His face. Jesus adds that He is a lamb now, but soon He will be the Lion of Judah. Who will fight against Him then? Understand that Jesus is speaking of what happened to Him in the past tense, yet at the time of these writings Jesus had not yet been born physically.

The most heartwarming response of Jesus to His Father came in when Jesus replied:

> Then I said, I have laboured in vain, I have spent my strength for nought, and in vain: yet surely my judgment is with the Lord, and my work with my God.
>
> —ISAIAH 49:4

Jesus had already been crucified (before He was born) and was wondering why the rewards of His suffering had not been manifested yet. Jesus was with God watching as the children of Israel in the Book of Isaiah were still rebelling against God! But God said:

> He shall see of the travail of his soul, and shall be satisfied: by his knowledge shall my righteous servant justify many; for he shall bear their iniquities.
>
> —ISAIAH 53:11

God was saying to His Son, "Hold on. You will see the results of your suffering unfold in the process of time."

When we read the accounts of Jesus's New Testament experience, of the Garden of Gethsemane, of the Crucifixion, we have to understand that the prophets in the Old Testament (Isaiah) not only spoke of this event as having already happened but Jesus Himself spoke of this event as having already happened. Understand that Jesus was born, He was alive, He was with God already before the foundations of the world. Genesis 18:1 speaks of the Lord's appearance to Abraham as one of three men. The Lord told Abraham that He was going to destroy Sodom because of the sin. In verse 22 we see that the angels went toward Sodom while Abraham continued to talk to the Lord. Genesis 18:33 ends by stating that the Lord went away. However, in Genesis 19:1 the angels went on to visit Lot.

What is amazing to me in this chapter is the fact that not only did God physically appear to Abraham in a fleshly form, but He and the angels ate food and drank while they were there. We know God's fleshly form is Jesus. What this simply means is that Jesus was not created before the foundations of the world metaphorically, but He was literally with God, walking, talking, and living with Him in heaven before the foundations of the world. He was God's Ambassador before He became Lord! Amazing!

Many great books have been made into movies, which is man's way of bringing a story to life. But this story is different. It is the movie before the book; it is life before it started; it is a "step by step" instruction manual for the life that we are now living. It is not only life in God, but it is life in me. It tells of my future in Christ, God's vision for me, and His plan for me. This is my life!

Like Jesus, the story of our life is foretold. I have already done that which I am required to do. I could not get out of it if I tried. That's why Scripture says that he who has begun a good work in you is faithful to complete it (Phil. 1:6). God can't abort what has already been birthed.

Jesus's death, burial, and resurrection had already been birthed in the spirit realm. However, it had to be birthed in the natural. The Scriptures say that our lives are hid in Christ (Col. 3:3). Our life has already been lived and our purpose and mission fulfilled in Christ. When Christ said, "It is finished," He meant that His redemptive work in us had been finished.

When we were chosen by God, we were sealed from that moment. The word that God spoke before the foundations of the world had been performed immediately after those final words were spoken. This is why our Lord tries to get us to understand that the battle is not ours. The struggle is not ours. Jesus endured the affliction of the Cross for us. It is foolish to attempt to imperfectly do something that has been already done in complete perfection.

The new and old prophets all have one major component in common. They loved not their lives unto death. Their aim in life was to do the will of the Father before the birth of Christ and proclaim the reality in the Old Testament that "the Word of God was made flesh," was crucified, buried, and rose for our redemption in the New Testament.

Chapter 2

THE AGONY "BEFORE" THE CROSS

W E TEACH ABOUT the Cross, Jesus's death, burial, and resurrection, and the emphasis on the need for Jesus's death so that we might have eternal life. But what about the period before the Cross? The Bible states that in the Garden of Gethsemane Jesus prayed to the Father three times to ask that this cup pass from Him.

> And being in an agony he prayed more earnestly: and his sweat was as it were great drops of blood falling down to the ground.
>
> —LUKE 22:44

THE AGONY *AND* THE CROSS

While I was in communion with the Lord, He revealed to me the pressure that was upon Jesus. The battle between Jesus's will and God's will presented so much pressure that the body was unable to physically or mentally process this phenomenon. It appears that Jesus's soul or will, in alliance with His body, literally fought with the Spirit of God in Him. His spirit was willing, but His flesh was weak. This is the law of the members in our body that Paul speaks about—Paul's will warring with his spirit for control of his body. Jesus's body was in an uproar during this time of battle, and every normal function of His flesh caused great pressure, resulting in a very rare malfunction that we refer to today as a malady.

The man Jesus prayed in agony that God might allow Him to escape the hard struggle, the mental and physical suffering that was required to purchase us back from Satan and restore eternal fellowship with the Father. It is important to note, however, that Jesus prayed that God would change His mind about the means, not the end. As with the men in the fiery furnace, Jesus was well prepared to endure this great affliction, should God not change His mind. Jesus was manifested that He might destroy the works of the devil, and He knew that this fate was not only the reason He was born; it was, more importantly, God's eternal will for Him.

I sought the Lord concerning the pain and agony I had been experiencing during my devotion with Him. When God calls us to ministry or to a special place in Him, especially one of dying, denying, or suffering, our flesh wars against our spirit for control of our will. We know that this fate is God's will for our lives, but we pray, "God, is there another way? Do I have to go this route? Can't I do it differently, with less suffering?" But God answers, "In this way is the Son of God glorified!" Although our spirit *wills* to please God, our flesh by nature does not want to yield to God. It is further made difficult by the demonic influences that seek to instigate or encourage our disobedience.

OUR CROSS

Like Jesus, we must bear our cross. Jesus said to take up your cross (Luke 9:23). In other words, "Do not run from the trials, tribulations, and tests (which represent your cross), but take them up, carry them, just like I did." When Jesus says, "....and follow me," He means, "...and do what I did. I did it for you. Now you must do it for someone else. This is a sacrificial race. Your life is not your own. I purchased you with my blood. Yet I do not treat you as a slave master treats his slave; I call you friend. I have shared my kingdom rights with you. I have purchased you for my work and for my glory, but unlike the worldly slave master, I am a rewarder of them that diligently seek me. I have riches laid up in heaven for you. If you do what I did, you will receive the same reward and blessing that I have. While it is true that Jesus has gone to prepare a place for you, that where He is, you may be also, He has done more; He has given you the Comforter, which is the Holy Spirit, to help you achieve every earthly goal that He has set before you."

Chapter 3

THE SUBSTITUTE AT THE
FOOT OF THE CROSS

I S THE FOUNDATION-TRUTH of Christianity the rock on which our hopes are built? It is the only hope of the sinner and the only true joy of the Christian—the great transaction, the great substitution, the great lifting of sin from the sinner to the sinner's surety, the punishment of the surety instead of the sinner, the pouring-out of wails of wrath that were due the transgressor upon the head of his Substitute, the greatest transaction that ever took place on Earth, the most wonderful sight that even hell ever beheld, and the most stupendous marvel that heaven itself ever executed.

> For he hath made him to be sin for us, who knew no sin; that we might be made the righteousness of God in him.
>
> —2 CORINTHIANS 5:21

What gives this occasion, this celebration its meaning? He is risen! He rose victoriously, and because we are in Him we are victorious as well. Christ's victory is our victory. Before we continue we must understand without a shadow of a doubt that we serve a risen Savior. Jesus also spoke to His disciples and said, "I am the resurrection, and the life" (John 11:25). The writer of Hebrews sums it up beautifully.

> Then said I, Lo, I come (in the volume of the book it is
> written of me,) to do thy will, O God.
>
> —HEBREWS 10:7

> By the which will we are sanctified through the
> offering of the body of Jesus Christ once for all.
>
> —HEBREWS 10:10

> For what the law could not do, in that it was weak
> through the flesh, God sending his own Son in the
> likeness of sinful flesh, and for sin, condemned sin in
> the flesh.
>
> —ROMANS 8:3

Simply, put a spotless Savior stands in the place of guilty
sinners. God lays upon the spotless Savior the sin of the
guilty so that He becomes, in the expressive language of
the text, sin. Then He takes off from the innocent Savior
His righteousness and puts that to the account of the once-
guilty sinner so that the sinner becomes the righteousness of
the highest and divine Source, the righteousness of God in
Christ Jesus.

> Wherefore in all things it behooved him to be made
> like unto his brethren, that he might be a merciful and
> faithful high priest in things pertaining to God, to
> make reconciliation for the sins of the people.
>
> —HEBREWS 2:17

> For such an high priest became [was fitting for] us,
> who is holy, harmless, undefiled, separate from sinners,
> and made higher than the heavens;
>
> —HEBREWS 7:26

In considering the great doctrine of substitution or the substitute, we can see that God man made a little lower than the angels crowned with glory and honor. Being over the works of God's hands with a heart and eyes that look up and see our sins laid upon Christ, at the foot of the cross we must find ourselves right now looking up at it with great adoration. First, at the foot of the cross we see God's justice, keeping in mind that when God's justice came to smite the sinner it found the Substitute, or Jesus, in the sinner's place, and justice smote him relentlessly, laying to the full the whole weight upon him. God's justice was set on saving our soul. Despite our sinful state, God would not be unjust even to indulge His favorite attribute, mercy. To save you and me, He would not tarnish His justice. God said that the soul that sins shall surely die (Ezek. 18:20). Yes, there was severe and unrelenting punishment and ultimate death for the sinner, but it was our Lord who bore it in my place. He was crucified for me.

Chapter 4

CHRISTIANITY OR DECEPTION

A S IT WAS with Paul, so it is today: Men are selling out for the temporary prosperity that comes from a devotion to a false doctrine. It is not the world that has instituted the deception in Christianity and has over the years publicly reinforced this travesty. It is the church. The church has taught us that if we are suffering, then we are out of the will of God and must be doing something wrong. That means that the Word of God as presented in Hebrews 5:8 somehow testifies that Jesus did something wrong, because it states that He did suffer. However, the Word of God tells us that even though Jesus was a Son, He learned obedience by the things that He suffered. How could this concept be true?

The Bible also declares that Jesus was without sin. So then, He was without sin, yet He learned obedience by the things that He suffered. Jesus suffered during the period that He was without sin. It was after Jesus's suffering in life that He suffered in death for our sins. If what the preachers are teaching about suffering is true—that there is sin in your life—then they are preaching a Jesus that they have concluded to be a sinner, have condemned, and therefore cannot possibly believe in.

The Scriptures declares that if someone died by hanging on a cross or tree, they were considered cursed by God. So the question the Romans posed was, How, then, could the

man they believed to be the Messiah die on a cross, signi-
fying that He was cursed by God?

> And if a man have committed a sin worthy of death,
> and he be to be put to death, and thou hang him on
> a tree: His body shall not remain all night upon the
> tree, but thou shalt in any wise bury him that day; (for
> he that is hanged is accursed of God;) that thy land be
> not defiled, which the Lord thy God giveth thee for an
> inheritance.
>
> —DEUTERONOMY 21:22–23

You see, the Romans were deceived, then, the same way
we are today. They believed in the Messiah, His deity, and
His Sonship until it came time for God to be revealed in
and through Him. This revelation must come by suffering
and humiliation. We believe the man or the woman to be of
God until it is time for God to be revealed in them through
suffering.

The deception: we do not see the *reason* these men and
women are suffering (like the children held captive in Egypt).
God said that He had hardened Pharaoh's heart so that He
might be glorified. We see the resistance of Pharaoh's way
before we see the glorification of God. The children of Israel
saw the fervent resistance of Pharaoh through their continued
suffering, which caused the children of Israel to doubt God.
They didn't see the "so that God would be glorified" part.

TRUE TRUST

The person who places their trust in man and not in Jesus
alone (without reasoning) will find himself deceived into
believing in, following, and respecting the man or woman
who does not portray a correct image of God. Satan can portray a false image of God in and through this person that is,

in fact, an image of himself. This can cause people to worship his image or him. This is precisely how the Antichrist will come into power.

> And they worshipped the dragon which gave power unto the beast: and they worshipped the beast, saying, Who is like unto the beast? who is able to make war with him? And there was given unto him a mouth speaking great things and blasphemies; and power was given unto him to continue forty and two months.
>
> —REVELATION 13:4–5

> And all that dwell upon the earth shall worship him, whose names are not written in the book of life of the Lamb slain from the foundation of the world.
>
> —REVELATION 13:8

This is why the Bible tells us to walk by faith, not by sight, because our senses will always mislead us. The ministry that insists that suffering in your life is a direct result of sin and simultaneously names the name of Jesus is a lie, and those that make this proclamation are deceivers.

> For there shall arise false Christs, and false prophets, and shall shew great signs and wonders; insomuch that, if it were possible, they shall deceive the very elect.
>
> —MATTHEW 24:24

Chapter 5

IS THIS THE CHRIST/OUR CROSS?

*Now when John had heard in the prison the works of Christ, he
sent two of his disciples, And said unto him, Art thou he that
should come, or do we look for another? Jesus answered and
said unto them, Go and shew John again those things which
ye do hear and see: The blind receive their sight, and the lame
walk, the lepers are cleansed, and the deaf hear, the dead are
raised up, and the poor have the gospel preached to them. And
blessed is he, whosoever shall not be offended in me.*

—MATTHEW 11:2–6

JOHN THE BAPTIST

JESUS SPOKE OF John the Baptist as the greatest man ever
born to woman. We know John as the man in the wilderness preaching the soon-coming Christ, baptizing and
preaching in preparation for the soon-coming King. This is
the man that lived on locusts and wild honey in the wilderness while boldly proclaiming the message of salvation. John
had been preaching for many years the impending arrival of
the Savior of the world, and finally there came the day when
He had come. I can imagine John proclaiming, "Finally He
has revealed Himself to me. I have seen Him with mine own
eyes. I have touched Him and have seen the glory of God
descend upon Him, and I have heard with my own ears as
God declared, 'This is my beloved son in whom I am well

27

pleased.' I have even had the awesome privilege of baptizing this God–man. So then why am I, a messenger of Christ, chosen by God, now finding myself in prison?" Now we see this same John questioning the deity of Jesus, asking, "Is this the One, or should I look for another?"

IS THIS A BOOK OF CONTRADICTIONS?

Many have attempted to persuade us in the period of great trials and tribulations that our prison experience is not from God. They so boldly use the Scriptures to declare to us that the God that they know would not hurt His people. God desires that we prosper and be in good health, even as our soul prospers (3 John 2). Surely this God would never expect us to endure trials and tribulations; He would only desire good for us and seek to give us joy unspeakable and full of glory in this life, to cause with the dawning of every new day excitement and ecstasy.

I have heard others speak of the Bible as a book of contradictions, that the Bible continually contradicts itself. Jesus speaks of the love of the Father and the disciples declare the freedom of the Lord for our lives, but we ignore or overlook the many warnings of martyrdom. The joy that the Bible speaks of is the joy *in* tribulation, *in* persecution. The Bible speaks of how we glory *in* infirmities.

It is not that the Word of God contradicts itself; it is the fact that often our self-centered nature wants to apply the glory lines of the Scripture to our lives while dismissing the truths of the persecution aspect. It is not that there is contradiction in the Word of God but that there is a misunderstanding in our perception of it. We know Daniel was in the lion's den, we know that the Hebrew boys were in the fiery furnace, we know that the apostle Paul wrote most of the

New Testament in prison, and we know that Stephen was stoned to death. However, we contribute the suffering of these men to our account. In other words, they suffered so that we don't have to.

MOMENTARY AFFLICTION

> For our light affliction, which is but for a moment, worketh for us a far more exceeding and eternal weight of glory.
>
> —2 CORINTHIANS 4:17

Now, according to this passage of Scripture, we have affliction. God did not say that our affliction was light, but that our affliction was light in comparison to the vast and transcendent glory and blessedness never to cease. These present afflictions are preparing us. Not only are they preparing us, but they are producing in us an everlasting weight of glory. It stands to reason that without the affliction and the persecution, we would not be prepared for the blessings of the Lord. Why?

Our flesh cannot please God. We know this in theory, but we do not know this in truth. Therefore, we spend our days attempting to do things that *we* have deemed acceptable and pleasing to God. If we continue to strive to please God in our mortal bodies, we will never be transformed by the spirit of God into the image of his Son.

So then, God must show us the failures in our attempts to please Him. If our righteousness is as filthy rags in the sight of God, then what in the world are our faltered attempts to please Him? If it is true that we cannot please God by the flesh (without a speck of sin), then how can we please Him in a sinful state? The Bible declares that all have sinned and come short of the glory of God, that if we say we have no sin, then we deceive ourselves (Rom. 3:23; 1 John 1:8).

29

God's ways are not our ways.

> And if they be bound in fetters, and be holden in cords
> of affliction; Then he sheweth them their work, and
> their transgressions that they have exceeded.

—JOB 35:8–9

TAKE NO OFFENSE

In the light of truth, we continually contradict the very words
of our Lord concerning us. Our pride allows us to believe that
we know the mind of God and his will for us through our
sinful and selfish interpretation of the Scriptures. Therefore,
when the truth of the Word of God is caused to be revealed in
and through us, we faint. So then we, like John, ask the question, "Are you the One, or should we look for another? I am
in prison. I was living better when I had a head-knowledge of
you. But now that I have become personally acquainted with
you, I have found myself in prison awaiting death. Is this the
Lord that I have been testifying of and selling my life out for?
I served You, but after I became personally acquainted with
You, I lost my children, I lost my mate, I lost my job, I lost
my friends. I didn't have a lot, but what I did have before was
better than what I have now. Tell me, Lord, what benefit have
You been to me?"

> And blessed is he, whosoever shall not be offended in me.

—MATTHEW 11:6

When we are confronted with the truth of the life of Christ
with respect to our sharing in His cross experience, we take
offense. This offense causes us to stumble. Suddenly, Jesus is
not who we thought He was. He is not the God of love, the
God of mercy, the God of deliverance. We now see Him as

the God of pain, sorrow, and agony. We therefore return to our old master, Satan, who deceptively promises us the life we expected God to give us. We become offended at Christ.

YOU WERE BOUGHT WITH A PRICE

We cannot glorify God in our bodies through our perception or comprehension of who He is. We cannot even begin to have a relationship with God without first understanding that He is God, and we were created to be used for His glory. Our life is not our own; we have been bought with a price:

> Ye are bought with a price; be not ye the servants of men. Brethren, let every man, wherein he is called [in every state], therein abide with God.
>
> —1 CORINTHIANS 7:23–24

God is the One who purchased you when you were discarded goods, when your life was void of any real joy, when you had no idea you were on a fast track to your eternal home, hell. When you were hopeless and helpless and not worthy to be purchased, God purchased you, and because our God takes the foolish things of the world to confound the wise, God uses the rejected and hopeless. God chose you when no one else wanted you. How do you, then, in arrogance, decide to take use of God's grace, love, and blessing for personal gain? We do not use the gifts of God for our purpose, but God uses the gifts He places in us for His purpose.

The same God who gifts us for His use will first break us to put us back together again His way, for His use.

When we can see the truth of the life, death, and resurrection of our Lord and Savior Jesus Christ, then and only then will we willingly submit our life, our will, and our body as a submitted servant to God. The Christian does not skip through the tulips in the worldly sense; we skip through the tulips in the knowledge that we have a crown laid up for us in heaven. We find excitement and glory in the fact that we have been chosen and found worthy to suffer for Christ's sake. We glory in our tribulation. We begin to understand and comprehend that Jesus did not come to bring peace, but a sword; to set a man at variance against his own household; that in reigning with Christ, we become an enemy to the world, to those who oppose Him. Like the apostle Paul, we experience a joy that's unspeakable and full of glory, and we see our life as unto Christ and death as our gain. We have a hope, which we cannot see. The Scriptures declare:

> For God is not unrighteous to forget your work and labour of love, which ye have shewed toward his name, in that ye have ministered to the saints, and do minister.

> —HEBREWS 6:10

Chapter 6

ISSUES OF THE HEART

A good man out of the good treasure of his heart bringeth forth that which is good; and an evil man out of the evil treasure of his heart bringeth forth that which is evil: for of the abundance of the heart his mouth speaketh.

—LUKE 6:45

OUR STOREHOUSE

THE BIBLE SPEAKS of the heart as a storehouse. This simply means that it is a place where something is stored. A man's treasure is that which he has stored up, be it a savings account, antiques, or trust fund. It is his riches, what he has placed a great deal of time, commitment, and energy into securing. The Bible refers to what is stored in our heart as treasure. What is treasure? Something of value to us that we have worked tirelessly to obtain.

So, in our storehouse (our heart, our will) we have hidden treasures. What is this great mystery, this concept? To understand this saying, one must be willing to go in depth, to go past their surface understanding and be prepared to deal with the hidden issues once they are revealed. Oftentimes people are afraid to see what is in them.

I can remember desiring to go deeper in the knowledge of Christ and simultaneously being afraid of what I would see once the issues of my heart were revealed. On the outside, I appeared to be a loving, caring, giving, patient, kind, and longsuffering person. But on the inside I was hateful, resentful, bitter, prideful, and all-around evil. I knew like no one else the issues of my heart, how they had affected me. I was a master at hiding what I wanted hidden and revealing only the part of me I wanted exposed. I knew how to forgive on the surface but inwardly remember the gory details of every evil that was done to me. I was continually on guard, especially against those who had revealed their own evils to me. I would smile but inwardly think, "You have no idea who you're dealing with." I was intrigued by the fact that people believed they had a handle on me when I knew all too well that they didn't have a clue.

I knew the issues of my heart. I knew what was in my storehouse, but it was the Holy Spirit who showed me the depths of the evil in me. Even when the reality of my heart was conveyed through angry words and violent acts, the imaginary me would deny the evidence. I refused to accept that I was who I was. It was after the Holy Spirit began to reveal me to me that I began to see the character that was embedded within me and the extent to which this character opposed the character of Jesus. I did not know why I could never get the victory over certain areas in my life, no matter how much I wanted to please the Lord. After He showed me my true self, I realized I was incapable of doing it. My heart was an abundance of evil, which warred like a man fighting for his very breath against the will and the character of Christ.

THE OLD CHARACTER

Many people have spent a great deal of time developing the character that they now have. Those who are angry, bitter, resentful, and spiteful did not just get that way overnight. Through a series of unpleasant circumstances or possibly out of the issues of an already established evil heart, the person has spent many years perfecting these evil qualities. Much time was spent dwelling on unpleasant and hurtful situations with thoughts of revenge. We see daily in the news and read in the newspapers of youngsters so driven by revenge that they go into the schools and shoot their fellow students. Oftentimes these are children who have been rejected, mistreated, insulted either by parents or classmates, or both. They have determined that they will get even and have spent a great deal of time calculating and then planning out their means of revenge. These children did not have a momentary memory lapse or an experience of temporary insanity. These acts were carefully planned and thought out.

The Bible declares that the evil or good in our hearts have been stored up. When one speaks through an abundance of love, or an abundance of hate, rest assured that what you are hearing is from their storehouse. If one threatens bodily harm, chances are that individual is quite capable of acting out these threats, because what was spoken has been at work in his or her heart for a long time.

This is why many of us must go through extensive deliverance. Although we want to please our Lord and Savior Jesus Christ, the evil within us, resulting from our sinful state and rebellion against God, will war against the regenerated spirit attempting to gain control of our life. Our heart must be purged. It must be changed. Until the change is complete, what comes out of our mouth from the storehouse "treasure," which has received deposits for some fifteen, twenty, thirty, or forty years, will be destructive.

Imagine the bank account of someone who has been placing one hundred dollars per month in a savings account for twenty years. That is twelve months times twenty years, which equals two hundred and forty deposits of one hundred dollars, or twenty-four thousand dollars. The one hundred dollars has multiplied itself two hundred and forty times in twenty years. If we have had deposited into ourselves a spirit of anger at age ten, by age thirty, twenty years later, that spirit of anger has multiplied in its intensity two hundred and forty times. Yes, we are capable of murder and many other heinous crimes. We have stored up a "treasure" of anger, but let us add insecurity, mistrust, resentment, and bitterness to the equation, and we have a major catastrophe waiting to happen. We are a walking destructive machine. Nothing in the root of that person is good, but all is evil.

SOCIETY'S VIEW OF NORMAL

Many people are normal in the eyes of society. They have wives, husbands, and children. They maintain jobs, some very good jobs. They attend our local churches and the PTA meetings. Some are daycare providers. One day they snap, killing innocent people, some of them children, and we are stunned! What in the world happened to this person? "He was so nice." "She spoke to me every day." "He helped me take out my trash and carried my groceries for me." "I would watch as she played with her children and went everywhere with them." What was the straw that broke the camel's back?

A person who stores up treasure for riches intends one day to use those treasures, whether to obtain a comfortable life financially or to pass it on to their children. A person who stores up treasures of hate intends to use the "arsenal" he has been storing up. When someone desires to please God in his or her flesh, that person comes to the realization that in order to please the Lord his or her character (or the treasures in his or her heart) must not only be transformed but most conform to the character of Christ. An individual cannot effectively use the treasures and the blessings of the Lord without having the mind of Christ to direct his or her paths in his or her distribution of these riches.

When Satan desires to use an individual for the destruction of others, he must first place his character within his or her heart. This comes through a series of destructive situations in that person's life. Over a period of years this person has been transformed and has conformed to the image of his or her master, Satan; now, it is time to distribute those treasures. The Holy Spirit's job in our life is to undo the character created in us by Satan by first disarming us. When a bomb has been placed in a certain place, before attempting to move the bomb, the bomb specialist will attempt to disarm it. If disarming it is not possible, then the bomb squad will attempt to set the bomb off but will first ensure that this process will not affect surrounding lives. The Holy Spirit will first attempt to disarm us. He knows that the enemy has been preparing us for destruction, and we are now at the point of being activated. We have placed bombs (or destructive behavior) in many areas, and these areas have been designated. Some of us have had abortions, several failed marriages, have committed murder and other hateful crimes, and have caused hurt to many people in our lives, oftentimes including our children. While all bombs have not yet been disarmed, those that would ultimately bring destruction to us have been.

THE HOLY SPIRIT BRINGS CONVICTION

It is now the goal of the Holy Spirit to bring conviction to our hearts for the destruction that we have already caused and to reverse the intent (the destructive forces), which has already been set in place for more destruction. This requires a character change, but our character has hidden evils in secret places. We must get to those hidden storerooms of evil one by one until all have been exposed and destroyed. The wonderful thing about our Lord Jesus is that once those hidden evil desires have been exposed the Lord purges those evils from our hearts and replaces them with the opposite character, His character. Once hate has been exposed and removed, love replaces it. Love is God, and God is love. This powerful force cannot be defeated.

Once the character of God has replaced the character of Satan, we are now an arsenal, a storehouse, of good. All that we say and do is good. All that we desire is good. All that we are (in Christ) is good, and this good comes from its source, which is love. Who is love? God is! Out of our belly shall flow rivers of living waters (John 7:38). Come, drink from this fountain of life and live. How wonderful it is to have previously been a fountain of death for all those who came into your path and to now be transformed into a fountain of life.

> For ye are bought with a price: therefore glorify God
> in your body, and in your spirit, which are God's.
>
> —1 CORINTHIANS 6:20

We have now become a useful tool for the Master, a fountain of life to which one can come and also live. Now, glorify God in your body!

Chapter 7

A PSALM OF PRAYER

David, Our Example

D
AVID, A MAN after God's own heart, spent a great deal of his life in prayer to the Lord, as recorded in the Psalms. We admire and are in awe at the eloquence in which he spoke. We use as a pattern the words of David in our own expressions to God. Sometimes when we do not quite have the words to express our feelings in a matter, we can rely on the Psalms to be able to touch our innermost feelings and relate our feelings effectively for us.

Oftentimes we neglect to research the life of David with respect to these prayers. We know that he was a man after God's own heart; we know that he was chosen out of the house of Jesse, the youngest and frailest of the sons; and we know that he defeated the giant with a slingshot. However, we skirt over the fact that the great exploits done by David as a child were a direct result of total trust in the ability of the Lord. David never bragged except to brag of his God. David knew as a child that he could do anything through God. He told the people that he would defeat the giant by the hand or the help of the Lord. As a boy, he did not at any point conjure in his heart that he himself was capable of defeating this giant, but he gave the credit to his God as the Empowerer.

David declared that he was young and now he's old, and

he's never seen the righteous forsaken or their seed beg-
ging for bread (Ps. 37:25). The Bible lets us know through
the Chronicles and by David's own prayers and songs that
throughout David's life he totally depended on God. It stands
to reason that God would choose him to become king. God
knew that He could trust David to carry out His ordinances
to a T! God knew that David would obey Him at all costs and
would be totally dependent on the Word of the Lord.

GOD'S PERMISSIVE WILL

God allows us over the majority of our life to build empires
just to show us how fragile they are. We use the best mate-
rials that we can get our hands on, and we are careful to
build a steady foundation. Some of us complete high school
and go on to college. Some of us excel in college and go on
to master's and doctorate programs. We find a good job, a
great mate, and have wonderful children. Just when all seems
to be going great, God will, at the foundation, move a loose
brick, and the whole structure will come crumbling down.
Our career, our family, our goals, our goods—gone!

In the natural, God would appear to be an unjust God.
"Why would the God I serve allow such a terrible thing like
this to happen to me? If God is a God of love and He desires
and wills that I prosper and be in good health even as my
soul prospers, then why did He allow such total destruction
in my life?" God is a God who above all desires that we be
reconciled back to Him, at all costs! God knows that this life
is temporal and that the eternal life is much more important. What kind of God would our Father be if He allowed us
to experience the joy, prosperity, contentment in and of this
life and then allow us to go to hell? But we ask the question,
Why can't we have both? The Bible clearly states that Satan is

the prince of this world. There is no way to be consumed or endowed with the fullness of the riches of this earth without somehow yielding in some way to its prince. That is why the Bible says that it easier for a camel to go through the eye of a needle than for a rich man to enter into heaven (Matt. 19:24).

THE WORLD AND THE CHRISTIAN

The world does not cater to the Christian. The world and its sin are targeted toward the sinner. The Christian who has enjoyment in this life is one who takes no thought for the things of this world. This person sees all things as an opportunity to glorify God and for God's glory to be revealed in and through these things. Only this person can be trusted with the world's riches.

THE HEART OF GOD

A man or woman with the heart of God wants prosperity for the purpose of expanding ministry to reach the lost for Jesus. These people want the joy to overflow out of them so that the love of Christ might be shown in their everyday lives. They want to show the peace of the Lord, which surpasses all understanding, so that those in their lives who knew of their past life in sin will know that truly there is a God. A man or woman with a heart for God detaches him or herself from the tangible things in the earth. These people are not content with a beautiful home and a fine care, not when there is still an unsaved soul out on the streets. They cannot sleep knowing that just four are saved; it's not enough. They say, "I want the Smiths' four saved and the Davises' four saved and the Franklins' four saved."

DAVID, THE KING

David's prayers continued to be recorded until his death. David did not stop praying after he became king and had everything in the world a man could ask for. Instead, his prayers changed as he grew or as he matured. His prayer was a constant prayer of deliverance.

You see, with prosperity there is an increased amount of temptation. One in power is tempted to simply command obedience, to become a dictator and to become callous to the needs of people around them. David's problems did not go away when he became rich and powerful; rather, they multiplied exceedingly. This burden now on the shoulders of David—one he never asked for, by the way—became increasingly heavy. David became a target for his enemy, Satan, and with a great arsenal of evil at his disposal Satan went after David with everything he had. There was no way that David could defeat his enemy without the help of the Lord, and David never lost sight of this fact.

I am at my best right now as I'm writing. I have never been better than what I am *now*, but it is but a speck compared to what I am going to be in Christ. The point is this: it is not until we begin to progress in the spirit that we begin to see the frailty of the flesh. The higher we climb in the spirit, the clearer the filth of our flesh becomes to us. The more God blesses us, the more accountable we become. The Bible declares that right now we see through a glass dimly (1 Cor. 13:12). As time goes on and as we progress in the Lord, more and more of the evil within us is revealed. Likewise, the desire to become more like Christ increases.

Bathsheba was neither the first nor the last woman David lusted after and desired; however, she was the first unavailable woman he wanted and had the "power" to get. As king,

David was able to order her husband, who was in the army, to the front lines to be murdered so that he would have the man's wife and keep the unborn child he produced with Bathsheba a secret. David saw the worst of himself, his true self, as he progressed in the spirit.

Oftentimes we ask God for riches and success, but God knows how we would prostitute the power he gives us without godly maturity. David had a reverence and a love for God at the time he had Bathsheba's husband killed, but he still did it. The thing that we in this generation feel is the answer to our woes, our problems, is the thing that causes men to commit some of the most heinous acts. It is likely such an act had not entered into David's heart as a poor man.

THE RENEWING OF OUR MIND

The mind must be regenerated (renovated, restored) before the progression in God begins. However, in the progression and based on our increased ability to see and understand, God commands and expects us to continuously come up higher. Paul states, "I press toward the mark for the prize of the high calling of God in Christ Jesus" (Phil. 3:14).

DAVID, A MAN AFTER GOD'S OWN HEART

David's heart and mind were set toward God before the progression started. However, through the progression his mind became increasingly bent toward the heart of God. There we find the reason that David was a man after God's own heart. Although David knew it before he became king, he realized even the more after becoming king that everything was nothing without God. What's amazing to me with respect to David and his son Solomon is that David knew it in his heart and Solomon learned it by his mind through the great wisdom that he had. Solomon was the wisest man in the world, and yet he concluded that all of life was foolishness. The Bible asks the question, What does it profit a man to gain the whole world and lose his soul? David knew and his son learned that success, victory, prosperity, and wisdom without God were foolishness.

Here we find the Psalms, the prayers of a humble man having the privilege of life on both sides of the fence and concluding that none matter without God. We find in the Psalms a man totally and completely dependent upon his God, a man who communed not with a God in theory but a real God who could do all things according to His will and purpose, and if He decided not to, that was OK too! David knew God as Father. The prayers of David are no less than conversations between a man and his Dad. The beauty of this wonderful man David is that in all things he remained a child of God.

Chapter 8

WITHOUT FAITH IT IS
IMPOSSIBLE TO PLEASE GOD

WITHOUT FAITH, IT is impossible to please God, because where there is no faith there can be no true obedience. The life lived in God though Christ is a life of faith. This life is not a life of the five senses but a life in the supernatural realm. There is no possible way of pleasing God through a life lived in and by the natural senses. The natural senses of a person, like Adam and Eve, can be deceived, and they may fall short of obedience to the will of God. However, the man who walks in the spirit has revealed to him the things of the spirit. The natural man cannot understand the things of the spirit because they are contrary one to another. We cannot walk in the spirit and the flesh simultaneously. Although Jesus was flesh, He did not live in the flesh but lived continuously in the spirit. Jesus lived through His sixth sense, if you will, the faith realm, a realm where nothing is visible but all things are created and ultimately appear. The person who lives in the flesh, the person who lives in the natural realm, the five senses, can never please God. It is only the man or woman of faith, not the person who believes strongly but the person who walks in the faith realm, the spirit, who can please God. It is only when we walk in the spirit that we do not fulfill or satisfy the lust of the flesh.

OUR ROLE

As born-again spirit beings, we operate on a different system. We are not moved by what we see, taste, hear, smell, or touch but by the operations or the systems in the spirit or unseen world. Our reality, therefore, does not exist within our sense systems but exists in the spirit realm.

Our purpose here as born-again Christians is to look at a situation, something that is happening in this earth's realm, and seek the Holy Spirit's direction for handling the situation in the spirit. There is a spiritual answer for every natural occurrence. However, we will never find the spiritual answer with our natural mind. We cannot think the spiritual answer up, because it will go against the logic of our mind. Therefore, we must seek the answer in, through, and by the Holy Spirit and apply the solution as given.

Why did Jesus spit in the dirt to make mud and place it over the eyes of the blind man? Why did Jesus send the disciples into the fish's mouth to get the tax money? Why did Jesus tell the man to go bathe himself in the pool of Bethesda? We can speculate on why Christ gave these instructions and get deep with it, but the truth is, it doesn't make common sense. God's answers or solutions to our problems will not make common sense, because God's ways are different from our ways. Therefore, we must, by faith, obey the Holy Spirit in His directives without question. We must obey what we hear, but if we do not have the ability to hear in the spirit then we will be incapable of obeying; thus, we will not walk by faith.

WALKING IN THE SPIRIT

The spirit realm has no boundaries. It is not limited by the five senses, time, or walls or any of the restrictions we have here on Earth. The fact that we cannot conceive a thing does not diminish its ability to be so. The flesh dictates to us what we will do and how far we will go through continuous limitations. The spirit has no limitations, and any and all things are possible through Christ. Our responsibility is to simply believe. The flesh is subject to the spirit in all things and must obey the instructions and directives of the spirit—not simply our own spirit but our spirit submitted to Christ.

We spend a great deal of time rebuking our flesh and trying to bring our bodies under subjection to Christ, but it is the spirit man submitted to Christ that does the work in our bodies.

> I beseech you therefore, brethren, by the mercies of God, that ye present your bodies a living sacrifice, holy, acceptable unto God, which is your reasonable service.
>
> —ROMANS 12:1

The Lord is not asking us to deny ourselves, our real selves, that is, our spirit man. He is telling us that the purpose for our physical bodies should be to provide a continuous available sacrifice, a sacrifice that is holy and acceptable to God. In the Old Testament only untainted animals were used for sacrifice. God had specific requirements for the animals that were sacrificed unto Him. So it is with our bodies. God has specific requirements for the sacrificial use of our bodies. It is only when our spirit is yielded to the lordship of Jesus Christ that our bodies will become sacrificial unto God: "Walk in the spirit, and ye shall not fulfil the lust of the flesh" (Gal. 5:16). Walk in the spirit and your body will become a living— not a dead, but a living—sacrifice unto God.

In order to walk in the spirit of God and with God, we must replace God's ways with our ways. We must replace the unseen for the seen. We must hear the words of Jesus and believe them. Jesus said that He said what He heard the Father say, and He did what He saw the Father do. Jesus simply modeled His Father. When we look at our children and our grandchildren, we are amazed at how much their ways are like ours. Our children and grandchildren simply mirror us; they do and say what they see and hear us do and say. The problem arises when we do not see or hear what our Daddy does or says. Then how can we follow? The answer is always found in the person of Jesus Christ. Our Lord came to show us in the physical realm an exact representation of our Father. Therefore, what Jesus said and did is what our Father said and did, which is what we are to say and do.

Jesus was submitted to the Father in all things, and yes, He was a living sacrifice unto God. We must be submitted to Jesus in all things. What things? Everything that is said to us and shown us in the Gospels. Like Christ we must become that living sacrifice. Will my flesh want to do this? Absolutely not! I must crucify my flesh, its dictates and its lust, and command it to submit to the Word of God, the Word that I eat, live, and breathe morning, noon and night. My food is to do the will of my father." What is my father's will? His Word. This Word becomes my food, and my food, my life source, is found in the will of my Father.

God's Word declares that the Comforter, the Holy Spirit, will lead and guide us into all truth. This truth can only be found in the person and embodiment of Jesus Christ.

Chapter 9

FALSE IMAGES

W HEN GOD SPEAKS to His people, He uses natural symbols to relay the message of the Spirit. Often-times, as with Daniel and Ezekiel, they give proph-ecies that they themselves do not understand. Of course, we know now that many of these prophecies were for centuries later. However, as with Ezekiel, when God told him to speak to the dry bones, God gave him a "symbolic" or "natural" comprehension of what he was saying in the spirit so that the prophet could effectively relate God's will and purpose to the people. Jesus was not just God Incarnate, the Son of God; He was a symbol (a human manifestation) of the spirit Person of God. Jesus was a human portrayal of the mind of God in a human form for the purpose of giving us a comprehensible understanding of God's nature so that when the Holy Ghost brought rhema, we would be able to connect the dots.

We must always remember that Satan is a copycat of God. Satan has studied God's ways and attempts to simulate God. He even appeared as an angel of light. He subtly portrays God in our lives with deception so that in believing we are obeying God, we in fact obey him.

> Know ye not, that to whom ye yield yourselves servants to obey, his servants ye are to whom ye obey; whether of sin unto death, or of obedience unto righteousness?
>
> —ROMANS 6:16

God's presence commands brokenness. No one can stand in God's presence and not fall prostrate before Him. Even when God visited the prophets (Moses, Ezekiel, Daniel and others) they had to be strengthened by God to withstand His presence so that they could hear from Him. The Bible tells us in Revelation that the angels in heaven worship the One who sits on the throne night and day. There is such awe and reverence in the presence of God that one is speechless and can do nothing but worship.

Satan desires the same type of reverence. Satan does not simply want us to yield our members to him; he wants our loyalty, our worship. He wants us to bow down before him in submission to him. He wants us in every area to worship and obey him as God has commanded us to do Him only.

GOD'S LOVE TOWARD US

The difference is, however, that God's love toward us draws us to a place of worship in Him. This worship, in spirit and in truth, is birthed out of an appreciation and overwhelming gratitude for the love that He has expressed toward us by His spirit.

> Herein is love, not that we loved God, but that he loved us, and sent his Son to be the propitiation for our sins.
>
> —1 JOHN 4:10

God loved us so much that He gave His only begotten Son. In the eyes of flesh, God appears to be an unrighteous God for murdering His own Son, but in the eyes of the spirit, God is such a loving God that He could place the punishment of a world on His own begotten Son. His Son, because He is as loving as His Father, is willing to accept the penalty for us. That's love! In the natural, if a loved one tells us, "Thus saith the Lord," and it hurts our flesh, we see that person as an enemy; however, when an enemy tells us wrong but satisfies our flesh, we see him or her as a friend. By the time many of us come to grips with the massive deception that has destroyed our lives, it is now time to leave this earth, our destiny having never been fulfilled.

The Bible declares that God's strength is made perfect in our weakness. God also says that it is no profit for a man to gain the whole world and lose his soul. God's first priority is our spirit, our soul. Satan encourages the strengthening of our flesh (which is enmity against God) so that the spirit man (led and directed by God) can be weakened. After pretending to be our friend and leading us away from God and out from under God's protection, Satan demands obedience by the threat of destruction. Because we have now become dependent upon Satan for success, for happiness, for prosperity, and have ultimately become slaves to him, our only hope for regaining our relationship to God through the Holy Spirit is through the destruction of our flesh.

The process that should have been a fairly smooth one has now become a struggle of life and death consisting of intense battle and possible destruction. In other words, once we are lured out of the safety or protection of God by the deception of Satan, we have no choice but to yield to Satan for our survival. How many of us would knowingly bow down our face to the ground and worship Satan? Very few, yet it is the "Satan in the people" that we bow down to and worship.

WORSHIPING AN IMAGE

We do not worship the God of the universe; we worship the image of God as portrayed by those we highly esteem. The children of Israel identified God as "the God of Moses, Isaac, and Jacob." They did not have a personal knowledge of God. They had an image of God by people who portrayed the image of the God they respected and, in fact, did serve. This is why Jesus said:

> Think not that I am come to send peace on earth: I came not to send peace, but a sword. For I am come to set a man at variance against his father, and the daughter against her mother, and the daughter in law against her mother in law. And a man's foes shall be they of his own household.
>
> —MATTHEW 10:34–36

Oftentimes in relationships between a man and a woman, it is the image of the person that we are attracted to, not the actual person. When the relationship is new, the person in our eyes is absolutely stunning. They have the perfect look, the perfect speech; their face seems to radiate, and love appears to exude from their being. They are attentive to all of our needs, and they go the extra mile. Their personality is identical to ours, and this relationship in every area is perfect. Of course, over a period of time, always after we have become "entangled," the real person emerges. The selfishness, the self-centeredness, the arrogance, the controlling and manipulating aspects of their personality are revealed. The face that appeared to be flawlessly beautiful now reveals the scars of many years of betrayal and deceit. The portrayal of light is really a deception, but we've now been sucked in. These manipulators, through our weakened flesh, command obedience from us in all areas. There is the threat of desertion if one does not submit to their demands, the withdrawal of affection and affirmation, which we have come to depend upon for our self-esteem, and the prospect of public humiliation in the admission of our own wrongdoing in having the relationship in the first place.

THE ILLUSION OF SUCCESS

The overwhelming desire for the image or projection of success is causing many to wax cold, to turn away from their first love and to follow other gods. We are seeking the "blessings" of God without becoming acquainted with the Source of the blessing Himself. We have a knowledge of the law of nature, the law of sowing and reaping, the law of giving and receiving, and the law works whether sin is committed or not. The flowers still grow in the springtime, and seeds planted in the ground and watered will still yield forth an increase. So yes, it is possible to have the tangible blessings of God but not God. Jesus said the day will come when many who are condemned will ask Him, "Didn't we cast out devils in your name?" (See Matthew 7:22.)

The Bible instructs us to walk by faith and not by sight because our senses will always mislead us.

> For there shall arise false Christs, and false prophets, and shall shew great signs and wonders; insomuch that, if it were possible, they shall deceive the very elect.
>
> —MATTHEW 24:24

The person who places his or her trust in man and not in Jesus alone without human reasoning can find himself deceived into believing in, following, and respecting a man or woman who does not portray a correct image of God. Satan can portray a false image of God in and through a man or woman that is in fact an image of himself, and in so doing he may cause people to unknowingly worship his image or himself. This is precisely how the Antichrist will come into power, through a man used by Satan or portraying the image of Satan. In worshiping this man, the people will inadvertently worship Satan himself.

> And they worshipped the dragon which gave power unto the beast: and they worshipped the beast, saying, Who is like unto the beast? who is able to make war with him? And there was given unto him a mouth speaking great things and blasphemies; and power was given unto him to continue forty and two months.... And all that dwell upon the earth shall worship him, whose names are not written in the book of life of the Lamb slain from the foundation of the world.
>
> —REVELATION 13:4–5, 8

> Know ye not, that to whom ye yield yourselves servants to obey, his servants ye are to whom ye obey; whether of sin unto death, or of obedience unto righteousness [right doing]?
>
> —ROMANS 6:16

Chapter 10

BUT I WAS IN THE HOUSE!

MANY BELIEVE THAT it is impossible for a Christian to be deceived. The apostle Paul is the epitome of someone who we would say was "in the house." Paul himself in the Book of Galatians states:

> For ye have heard of my conversation in time past in the Jews' religion, how that beyond measure I persecuted the church of God, and wasted it: And profited in the Jews' religion above many my equals in mine own nation, being more exceedingly zealous of the traditions of my fathers. But when it pleased God, who separated me from my mother's womb, and called me by his grace, To reveal his Son in me, that I might preach him among the heathen; immediately I conferred not with flesh and blood: Neither went I up to Jerusalem to them which were apostles before me; but I went into Arabia, and returned again unto Damascus. Then after three years I went up to Jerusalem to see Peter, and abode with him fifteen days.
>
> —GALATIANS 1:13–18

THE APOSTLE PAUL

The Bible lets us know that the apostle Paul, or Saul as he was known before his conversion, was a devoutly religious man. He did not simply grow up in the church as a little boy and learn by example from those around him, but as we would put it in our language today, he went to Bible school.

Not only that, but Saul excelled over his classmates. He knew not only his genealogy backward and forward, but he knew the mind of God as taught in the Old Testament. He knew the meaning of the Commandments and the instructions received by Moses from God. He emphatically believed that every word written by the prophets of old was from God.

God had moved the church, the world from a state of accountability by the law to a state of unconditional love through grace through His Son's death. In the mind of Saul, this very thinking was not only contrary to the Word of God written in the scrolls but was pure evil. Saul actually believed that these "reformed" Christians were defiling the holy ordinances of God. One can see that Saul was not only passionate in his beliefs but believed he actually had "the Word of God" to back up his feelings.

Oftentimes in the church, the preacher gives an interpretation of the Word of God as written in the Bible. Even if there are questions in our spirit about that interpretation, we settle the statements made by this person as truth because we have seen what he is saying in the "scroll," or the Bible. Look, for example, in Deuteronomy 21:22–23:

> And if a man have committed a sin worthy of death, and he be to be put to death, and thou hang him on a tree: His body shall not remain all night upon the tree, but thou shalt in any wise bury him that day; (for he that is hanged is accursed of God;) that thy land be not defiled, which the Lord thy God giveth thee for an inheritance.

Now, it is clear that Saul, knowing the Scriptures in detail, fully learned in them, knew that this Jesus was crucified in Old Testament terms by being hung on a tree, so naturally He was cursed by God. To his view, those who would follow the teaching of this Christ obviously were not only in willful rebellion but had chosen idolatry. What Saul did not understand until it was revealed to him by God is that this Christ's death, this curse placed on Him, was not His curse but ours, that by His shed blood He redeemed us from the curse of this very law which Saul so aggressively defended.

CONTRADICTION OR CONFIRMATION

Many have spoken of the Bible in reference to contradictions. Like many others, Paul himself experienced this contradiction firsthand to the point that he found it necessary to retire into Arabia to get some understanding. "This Jesus is real. I saw Him with my own eyes. He restored my sight, but what about the Law? What about the Word of God, the instructions, the scroll passed down from generation to generation? The apostles will not be able to help me with this one. They believed all along. They don't have the answers to the questions in my heart."

Obviously, no man could satisfactorily answer the questions that Paul had. Only Jesus Himself could bring understanding to an obvious contradiction with understanding so profound as to cause Paul to defend this new understanding with the same zeal and energy he used to defend the Law— and even more, to the point of submitting his life even to execution. God is wise and all knowing, and there is a purpose for all that He does.

He placed the enthusiasm and zeal in Paul. He placed the incredible wisdom and the articulation in him for His own purpose. Why couldn't God just raise him up to use him, like he did John the Baptist? Why does God allow us to build the building for the purpose of tearing it down? As was the case with Moses, I suspect that one does not know or fully comprehend their natural inabilities until they have exhausted their natural abilities.

Men and women are funny. Our brains work totally differently. For most men, everything is black and white, but a woman can always find the gray area. Many times men, when looking for a location they've never been to, will read the map, go around in circles many times, and spend hours on a thirty-minute trip. A woman will simply pull over into the gas station and ask someone. So it is with God. If we just simply ask Him, we can get the answer a lot faster; but God gave us a will, and boy, do we exercise it. So there you have it: Paul would likely not have listened anyway, so God allowed him to go all around the mulberry bush.

It is important to note, however, that Paul's ignorant zealousness would later be used by God. God always looks for an opportunity to show mercy. We can be confident that all things will work out for good for those of us who love Him and are called according to His purpose. God had planned all along to reclaim Paul's great wisdom, his zeal, and his enthusiasm, which, although distorted, was bestowed by God in the first place. In reclaiming His imparted gifts to Paul, God would use it for His glory and to advance His kingdom.

Chapter 11

UNREASONABLE EXPECTATIONS

I N MY FAILED marriages, I believed that my husband gave 25 percent to my 100 percent, and as a result, my anger has been continually kindled by this perceived injustice and apparent neglect. The men were confessed Christians, one a pastor, and yet in my view they did none of what the Word of God instructs them to do as husbands. My continuous demands on them to be who and what the Word of God declares they should be have brought me much pain, sorrow, anger, and disappointment. I have expected these men to be men striving to become who God says they should already be, and have found myself sorely disappointed when the manifestation did not come.

THEIR ABILITY OR MY EXPECTATION

The real problem was in my expectation, not their inability. Jesus did not expect simply because He knew what was in man. Jesus told Peter that he would deny Him three times before the cock crowed thrice. When this actually happened, it wasn't Jesus who was surprised; it was Peter who was surprised at himself not discerning what was in his own heart. We spend so much time trying to get people to see the "stuff" inside of them. What we don't realize is that the "stuff" in them will testify of itself. The condemnation that comes from the enemy is enough punishment in and of itself without our adding to the sting of the self-exposure through finger-pointing.

We often get involved in relationships with people who appear to possess strength in areas that we do not. We can see in them benefits to our own life, and we see pieces to our own puzzle in them. When we become united with that person, it is with the expectation of having that missing or empty area in us filled. When this does not happen, we become angry, bitter, and vindictive.

On the contrary, Jesus never asked for or expected anything from anyone. The only request recorded in the Gospels is when Jesus asked Peter if he loved Him. When Peter answered yes, Jesus asked him to prove it by feeding his sheep. The Bible tells us to owe no man anything but to love him (Rom. 13:8). Jesus never spoke in the area of our receiving except to make reference to our receiving from God spiritual blessings now and heavenly blessings later. Jesus never misleads us to believe that we would receive back the good that we give to others. What about the scripture that declares, "Give, and it shall be given unto you…" (Luke 6:38)? In context, our reward is from heaven, not from men. From that same scripture we read, "With the same measure that ye mete withal it shall be measured unto you again." Simply stated, we will reap what we sow, and it is God who provides the harvest.

THE MARRIAGE COVENANT

One of the greatest distortions in history is that of the marriage covenant. What began as the most blessed relationship or union between people has resulted in one of the most destructive. The primary reason that the divorce courts are so full is simply that there has been an illusion regarding marriage. We read over and over about the marriage covenant, the institution of marriage, and how the order in marriage pleases God. The apostle Paul gives us so many instructions and directives concerning marriage; however, what should be and what is are two very different things. We want to live in the glory of the "should be" while allowing ourselves to be destroyed by the "what is." Every story in the Bible was printed for our instruction and direction. The Word of God is for the purpose of helping us understand ourselves. In order to understand marriage and relationships in general, you must go back to the beginning, when the relationship was first initiated, instituted, destroyed, and redeemed.

THE RELATIONSHIP COVENANT

We all know of the angel in heaven whose name was Lucifer who would later be referred to as Satan. Lucifer was overcome with pride and consequently decided that he would exalt himself above God. Of course, he and one-third of the angels were defeated. Satan and his fallen angels were cast out of heaven into what we now know as hell and were given authority over the earth for a period of time. Why did this happen? It happened because Lucifer broke the covenant relationship between himself and God. God created man in His image and likeness because He wanted to have relationship with him. God made man from the dust, breathed life into him, and gave him the created earth, complete with everything needed for a glorious life. The fallen angel, Satan, convinced man to rebel against God. Who did this evil angel convince?

The Bible does not tell us how long Adam was a single man, but I believe it was for a while. For God to decide that it was not good for man to be alone, and I would imagine that this conclusion came after observing Adam with the animals over a period of time. One must conclude that while Adam was a single man the enemy was unable to successfully conquer him.

SINGLENESS OF HEART

Adam was a single man, created by God and totally dependent upon God. His heart was to his God, and there was no competition. Then God created a woman who was beautiful and desirable to Adam. Now, Adam's emotions were split. He had a reverence and a spiritual love for God, but now the physical element had entered into the picture. Adam "desired" his wife, and this desire awakened emotions in Adam that he had not before experienced. Finally, Satan could find a weakness, a physical door. Let us set up the attack!

I think that it is important to note here that the Bible declares that sin found occasion through the Law. However, in the case of Adam and Eve, there was no Law to break, so what was the source of their sin? It was the same sin as Lucifer, pride. Like Satan, they shifted ultimate confidence from God to self.

In contrast, humility is the direct opposite of pride; humility depends solely on God's righteousness for salvation. There you have it, the root of all sin, pride. The reason Jesus was without sin is that He did what He saw the Father do, and He said what He heard the Father say. His food, His existence, His sustenance was to do the will of the Father. Pride does not exist in a spirit of humility that places obedience to the Father as its reason for existence. Jesus never shifted ultimate confidence from God to Himself, and thus sin could find no occasion and thereby had no door.

TAKING RESPONSIBILITY

We know that Eve ate the apple and then gave it to her husband to eat. We also know that their eyes were not opened when Eve at the apple; they were only opened after Adam ate it. Although the Bible states that they became one flesh, they were still two individuals. One of them could not bring the curse of sin upon both of them; it was needful that they both sin to bring forth the curse. We are so convinced or deceived into believing that if one spouse does not obey God the curse of God will fall, and our prayers will be hindered. Once one spouse sins, we just toss the blessings out of the window. We conclude that the thing that we have believed God for will never come to pass because of the unwillingness of the one spouse to obey the Word of God.

Again, Adam's and Eve's eyes were not opened until both of them ate the fruit. Understand that the enemy's tactic involves attacking the one spouse and causing him or her to lure the other into the trap. This is possible because our attempts to fix and control our own lives are always within the confines of a sinful, selfish, and self-centered motive. Consequently, we have unreasonable expectations of the fulfillment of God's ordinances by our mate.

It is for this reason Jesus said:

> Think not that I am come to send peace on earth: I came not to send peace, but a sword. For I am come to set a man at variance against his father, and the daughter against her mother, and the daughter in law against her mother in law. And a man's foes shall be they of his own household. He that loveth father or mother more than me is not worthy of me: and he that loveth son or daughter more than me is not worthy of me.
>
> —MATTHEW 10:34–37

63

The apostles fill the Word of God with instructions from the Ten Commandments in the Old Testament to the examples of Jesus in the New Testament on how to live godly lives. God knows that these instructions are impossible to follow in the flesh. Every order instituted by God is hated by flesh, and the flesh seeks ways to defy God. The flesh is enmity against God. In order to understand and conquer our flesh, to refuse to obey the dictates thereof, we must understand how the flesh works.

THE FLESH

The flesh is an entity created to be controlled. It is like a computer, containing numerous amounts of information and knowledge, but the computer operator must learn how to use this awesome tool. We are spirit beings, having been given a human or fleshly body to dwell in with a soul or mind to control the body's operations, yet we have no idea how to use it. The flesh was created in a perfect state, and the operation of this incredible system was to be taught by its creator. Unfortunately, our flesh, through sin, has become independent of its creator (God). Understand that Satan has been studying this tool, the human body, since its inception and has gained knowledge into its operating system. Although we were created in the image and likeness of our creator God, our flesh seeks to reprogram itself into the image of its new master, Satan. Why? Satan has deceived us into believing that God did something wrong, that He made a mistake in programming and left out the "enjoyment chip"; therefore, we ignorantly turn to Satan for repair and, as a result, are reprogrammed by him.

This sinful state opposes God and God's ordinances. We willingly submit ourselves to Satan through sin. To change ownership, we must willingly give ourselves back to our original owner, God. The problem is that while under the rule of Satan we were reprogrammed to receive his character. We are attempting to get a word processing program called Word Perfect 5.0 to operate effectively and efficiently in its new program, Microsoft Word 2000. We are attempting to get the character of God to work and operate within the confines of the character of the devil. We want the Spirit of God operating in and through us on our fleshly terms. Impossible!

This process of change within ourselves to be reprogrammed into the character of God is so difficult and so stressful that to lighten the burden we attempt to get outside help to assist us in our transformation. We know in theory that God is able and wants to do it, but we can't see him. We therefore shift the focus of our assistance from the God we can't see to the man we can see. Ah, we step into idolatry without even knowing it.

THE DELUSION

We speak of the term babe in Christ. We give people a shallow definition of the meaning of this term. We tell them that they are now born again, a new creature, and that God is going to transform them into His image if they simply read their Bible, come to church, and pray (although they have no idea how to pray). What we neglect to tell them is that as a child of God they will have to make a transformation that will, at times, cause them to feel like they are losing their mind. We don't tell them that all hell is going to break loose, and we definitely don't tell them that if the spirit of God does not recreate them before they get married and/or have children, then their hell will become their family's hell. We are a generation of people who preach and teach a "microwave gospel," a three-step program, and when people get discouraged and leave the church within a month or three, we wonder why! Many church leaders are drawing men and women into their churches and setting them up for the greatest failure of their lives, and these leaders too shall have their part in the lake.

> For which of you, intending to build a tower, sitteth not down first, and counteth the cost, whether he have sufficient to finish it? Lest haply, after he hath laid the foundation, and is not able to finish it, all that behold it begin to mock him, Saying, This man began to build, and was not able to finish.
>
> —LUKE 14:28–30

OUR DIRECTION

When attempting to reach a particular destination that is totally unfamiliar from a set point, one needs a map. If I want to drive to Texas from California, I must identify exactly where I am located in California to know how to get to the area in Texas in which I want to go. However, if I do not have a concept of north, south, east and west, I will not be able to read the map. In order to have this concept, I must have been taught at least that the sun rises in the east and sets in the west. In order to be taught, I must have received some education somewhere.

Even the ability to read the map symbolizes some form of education. I did not just wake up one day in infancy and start speaking and understanding. There was a process of development in which I first had to learn to talk, hear, and comprehend. There is no way I could comprehend north and south before first understanding the alphabet.

We instruct people in their lives in the way that they should live, and we "pull out" the Word of God to show them that what we are saying is correct and that we can prove it. The problem is not that they don't believe what you are saying. They believe you; they see it in black and white. But, all of their "willing" doesn't seem to make what they read come to pass in their life. We are trying to get an infant to understand north and south. It is impossible!

Ministers of the gospel spend so much time and energy trying to prove their superiority in speech and etiquette that they do not realize that what they are saying is going in one ear and out the other. It is absolutely impossible to understand spiritual truths of God without the Spirit of God having been placed within you.

GOD'S SPIRIT

In order to have the Spirit of God placed within us, we must realize that we need it. "If I have a great job, a good marriage, wonderful kids, and a savings account, why do I need this God? My emotional needs are met in every area of my life. Why do I need God? Is this God of love supposed to come and replace my wonderful existence? Is this the God I want? My husband gives me all the love in the world; I do not need to seek it from a 'spirit' I cannot even see!" What then is our response?

The Spirit of God, the Holy Spirit, goes into the inner being of a person, into the depths of his or her soul. He brings to the foreground those hidden issues of their heart and causes them to address those issues. The Bible declares, "It is not by might, nor by power, but by my spirit, says the LORD of hosts" (Zech. 4:6). As long as we have sufficient replacements (such as spouses, children, friends, prosperity, or followers), we will never see the need for Jesus. If we don't see the need, then we cannot receive the change, the deliverance. What happens when our support source is gone? What happens when the wife or husband is gone or when the children go away or those who support you and make you feel good are gone? What happens when you are all alone, and all you have is you? What do you do with what you are forced to see?

Every man of God in the Bible greatly used by God had a wilderness experience. During their testing period, many had no wife, no children, no houses, jobs, support groups, or congregations. They had no one. We have convinced ourselves that God is doing this mighty work in the one-day experiences that we have with Him, and unfortunately, we find out before the week is over that there is still a great deal more to be done in us. I believe that our biggest fear is the fear of being alone with God and, like a movie screen, seeing who we really are—not who we are in the particular situation, but the whole of our person. Could we stand to see the constant thoughts of evil, the selfishness, the bitterness, the unforgiveness, strife, and covetousness? Until we come to grips with ourselves, our sinful nature, and purpose in our heart to wrestle with it like Jacob and to walk in the spirit like Paul, we will continually exhaust the people in our lives with our impossible expectations.

This flesh can never be satisfied; therefore, it must be crucified. Our spirit, which searches for a resting place, can only find it in Christ, but our soul must make the choice once and for all. When finally we have purposed to put all of our energy, our thoughts, and our flesh under the submission and authority of the Holy Spirit, not being satisfied with anything less than the character of Christ in our person, then and only then can we have successful relationships with other people. Jesus could not be disappointed by the flesh because He put no trust in it.

Chapter 12

BEWARE OF SELF-VINDICATION

R ATHER THAN ACCEPT the verdict of guilty and plead for mercy, we choose to defend ourselves; therefore, God accepts our plea and allows us to go to trial. Though Jesus was accused, He opened not His mouth, and for every pain He responded with love. He who was perfect and committed no sin, He who was not guilty when accused, opened not His mouth and never defended Himself. We, on the other hand, continually defend ourselves in the face of the overwhelming evidence of guilt.

THE PUBLIC DEFENDER

It is the attorney's job, the public defender's job, to prove the innocence of the known guilty in the face of the over-whelming evidence against him. This attorney must convince these jurors (people having the ability to see the guilt clearly) that what they are seeing is misconstrued. In other words, it looks like a duck, it quacks like a duck, but it's not really a duck. How often the innocent are sent to prison because of an inadequate defense team, and how often the guilty are set free because of a convincing argument.

This same Jesus who did not attempt to defend Himself when falsely accused now sits at the right hand of the Father making intercession, pleading on behalf of the guilty. We spend the majority of our lives trying to prove our inno-cence and vindicate ourselves. What's more, we attempt to get others to validate the lie of innocence that we believe about ourselves.

JACOB'S WRESTLING MATCH

Jacob wrestled with the angel (with the Lord), and it was at the end of this great struggle that the angel asked Jacob what his name was. You see, Jacob was attempting to get God to vindicate him and bless him in spite of himself; however, in the midst of this great struggle, with every tug and pull, God was showing Jacob himself. At the end of the struggle, finally, Jacob saw himself and confessed his name was "Deceiver."

Our greatest aim in life is not to be successful in business, not to be wealthy, not to purchase a home, or drive a great car, nor is it our aim to be known for raising wonderful children. Our primary goal in life, the one we spend the most effort and energy on, is in attempting to convince people and ourselves that we are not the people that the God in us tells us we are. It is amazing to me how people (most not spiritual) can see the "real" us. While we may still be able to fool some and even ourselves, we are certainly no surprise to God. He knew before we were born who we are in the flesh, and while our primary aim is to prove to others and ourselves that we are not this wretched person, God is simultaneously trying to show us that we are.

What does all of this mean? It means that we have elevated ourselves to God's level and have decided to be our own judge and discount what God says about us. What's more, we are trying to get God to agree with us by blessing us in our current state. Through the wrestling circumstances in our lives, God is attempting to show us that He cannot bless us in this "fantasy" state, because the blessings we seek would not only cause us to become more puffed up but would ultimately destroy us. We would never experience the spiritual blessings; therefore, our request to God to skip the spiritual and get on with the natural has been denied. God is a spirit, and they who worship Him must worship Him in spirit and in truth. This means that our relationship with God must develop and be cultivated in the spirit. In the spirit, or in God's presence, truth is revealed. It was in the spiritual battle Jacob encountered with God that truth was revealed and a confession was made.

THE CONFESSION

When one is accused of a crime and faces a judge in court, that person is ordered to enter a plea for the crime of which they are accused. The plea is either guilty, not guilty, or no contest. If the plea is not guilty, immediately the case is set for trial. However, in some cases a confession is made that eliminates the lengthy process of a trial, and mercy is sought in exchange for the confession.

After a lengthy battle with the angel, Jacob confessed that he was a deceiver. It was at the point that Jacob confessed he was a sinner that God was able to bless him. He confessed! A righteous man in God's eyes is a man who has confessed that he is a sinner, has confessed his transgression, has without a jury condemned himself by the Word of God, and has cried out for mercy through Jesus Christ. "Yes, I am guilty. No need of a jury. I will just throw myself at the mercy of the court. I do not want an attorney to argue my case. I am not going to represent myself. My plea is 'guilty,' and my request is mercy in judgment."

THE TRIAL

It is sad to witness the trial of a rapist. In arguing the case on behalf of the rapist, the attorney for the rapist must show the victim as a criminal. He must convince the jury that this poor woman was in some way "asking for it." He goes into the woman's past and causes her to relive the abuse she suffered as a child. He insists that although a child, she could have stopped her adult abuser but didn't because she enjoyed the attention the abuse gave. In bringing this child to adulthood in the eyes of the jury, he shows that her past of prostitution, which was a direct result of her low self-esteem and her need to be validated by men, was a desired lifestyle and proof of her continuing need for male attention. This lifestyle was one into which she flung herself joyously. He convinces the jury that this man beating her while he raped her was something she wanted because in her life of prostitution, her pimp beat her, and she enjoyed it, as proven by her refusal to leave him. The attorney convinces the jury that she needed to be overpowered because it gave her the sense of security similar to what she experienced when her father did it. In short, this attorney has convinced this jury that this woman, in every sense of the word, asked for and enjoyed every part of this violent act by this man, not rapist.

Not only did this man abuse her, not only did her accuser, the attorney, replicate and remind her of the abuse she experienced in her childhood, but he has also managed to convince the jury—other people—that she was primarily responsible for this heinous act against her. This woman is now worse off than she was before, more damaged than ever, and she is now questioning whether or not what they are saying about her is true. This innocent woman, at the mercy of someone else's vindication, has become guilty.

As in the case of the Pharisees attempting to vindicate

themselves in the crucifixion of Christ, this attorney, in an attempt to vindicate his client, condemns and emotionally crucifies this poor woman. The purpose of this painful trial was simply to vindicate a man who was totally and completely guilty at someone else's expense. As awful as it sounds, a person in an attempt to vindicate him or herself will do this same thing at the expense of others.

ACCEPTING RESPONSIBILITY

God knows that if we do not accept responsibility for our own actions, we will destroy each other in an attempt to vindicate ourselves. This is why Jesus gives us the command to love each other as ourselves, esteeming each other higher than ourselves, because outside of this circle we will by nature destroy each other.

The Bible declares, "Greater love hath no man than this, that a man lay down his life for his friends." Which of us is willing to lay down our life rather than protect it for someone else? Which of us is willing to accept the blame to release another from the responsibility and the guilt? Which of us is willing to take the judgment for ourselves, let alone for someone else? I know of only one, and His name is Jesus.

THE BLAME GAME

When God approached Adam about breaking the command that God had given him, Adam's first words were, "The woman whom thou gavest to be with me" (Gen. 3:12). Immediately, in attempting to vindicate himself, Adam condemned and accused his wife, the woman created from his rib, his other half. He would sacrifice her up to save his own skin. No doubt, had there been some negative experiences in their lives up to this point, Adam would have pulled the covers off of her and exposed the hidden things in her past to further prove his point of her guilt. Eve in turn directs the blame to the serpent: "The serpent beguiled [tricked] me, and I did eat" (Gen. 3:13). From the beginning, in his attempt to vindicate himself, man has done so by placing blame.

THE FACE IN THE MIRROR

In this struggle in life to be validated, we frustrate others and ourselves. In the end Job repented in sackcloth and ashes, stating, "I have heard of thee by the hearing of the ear: but now mine eye seeth thee. Wherefore I abhor myself, and repent in dust and ashes" (Job 42:5–6). It was after his confession and deliverance that Job was in a position to pray for his accusers and received God's renewed success and blessing for his life.

The Book of Job deals with an execution of judgment on Job and his attempt to vindicate himself. It took forty-two chapters for Job to come to the conclusion and agree with God that he was, in fact, guilty and repent. This revelation about Job immediately wrought in Job a spirit of compassion for others, and in response to God's instruction, he gladly prayed for his accusers. Although men were guilty of false accusation against Job, God's primary concern at this point was for Job to see himself. God wanted this righteous man, this judgmental man, not only to see himself but to understand that it is God alone who judges.

Unlike man and the natural court system, God does not condemn some to vindicate others. All have sinned and come short of the glory of God; there is none righteous, no not one. (See Romans 3:10, 23.) It was this new heart for others in the face of God's grace toward him that caused the blessings of God to overtake Job. "It's me, it's me, it's me, oh Lord, standing in the need of prayer."

Chapter 13

THE BETRAYAL

P ETER TOLD JESUS that he would die for Him. Jesus responded, "Peter, before the cock crows thrice you will deny Me." Peter responded, "No, Lord, never!" More often than not, judgments that are made against us by people we know are not a result of something we did to them. It is simply that we have been betrayed by those we least expect simply for personal gain. We have taken the word of the one who has committed his or her life to us only to later be crushed by the reality that that person's words were just that—words. The Bible not only instructs us to put no trust in man but also entreats us not to put any trust in our own flesh, for the flesh is wicked.

It is God who searches the hearts of men, and only God knows the thoughts and intents of it. It is God who knows our motives, while our words dictate otherwise. Even our expressions, our convincing, and to some extent, we ourselves believe in the commitments that we make. It is a devastating thing to find out that the one to whom you've given so much of yourself would betray you for thirty pieces of silver, or that someone would deny even knowing you:

> When Judas, who had betrayed him, saw that Jesus was condemned, he was seized with remorse and returned the thirty pieces of silver to the chief priests and the elders. "I have sinned," he said, "for I have betrayed innocent blood." "What is that to us?" they replied.

"That's your responsibility." So Judas threw the money into the temple and left. Then he went away and hanged himself.

—MATTHEW 27:3–5

NO SURPRISES

Not only was the situation with Peter and that with Judas of no surprise to Jesus, but Jesus knew that these things must happen in order to fulfill the purpose of God in His life. It was needful for Peter to deny Jesus.

Then he began to call down curses, and he swore to them, "I don't know the man!" Immediately a rooster crowed. Then Peter remembered the word Jesus had spoken: "Before the rooster crows, you will disown me three times." And he went outside and wept bitterly.

—MATTHEW 26:74–75

Later Jesus would tell His disciples, "Go tell his disciples and Peter" (Mark 16:7, emphasis added), a depiction of God reconciling the world unto Himself. You see, it was the love and forgiveness of Jesus toward Peter that caused him to desire to never disappoint Jesus again. The reconciling love of Jesus produced the greatest apostle in history, and it is a revelation of that love for us that produces a life of holiness in us.

IN THIS IS LOVE

When that cock crowed its final crow, Jesus, without mumbling a word, simply turned around and looked at Peter. It is our nature when mistreated to attempt to defend ourselves against the one who hurt us. We want to rub it in that person's face and make them feel the pain that they have caused us, and we want them to repent over and over until we are satisfied in their sincerity. I believe the look that Jesus gave Peter was a look that said, "Peter, it's OK. I still love you."

I am reminded of the time when I was battling in court with my son's father for custody of my son. I heard him speak horrible things about me as he was instructing his attorney to fight dirty to win! I was so hurt that I had no response. I believe that if I had attempted to defend myself, I probably would have just cried. This was a man to whom I bore a son! Can you imagine denying someone openly when privately you proclaimed such love and commitment for that person? Can you imagine having that person turn and look at you with such love that says, "It's alright. I forgive you!" It wasn't the constant reminding of the fault; it wasn't the anger toward Peter; it was the expression and aura that said, "No matter what, I love you," that transformed Peter's life.

It is apparent that it is the one in whom we have placed the most love and attention who in turn can betray us. Why? Because God is trying to get us to a point where we say, "No matter what, I love you. No greater love a man has than to lay down his life for a friend."

I AM A PARTAKER IN CHRIST'S SUFFERING

Jesus said, "No one takes my life, but I lay it down." (See John 10:18.) Jesus willingly suffered pain and humiliation for us. Isaiah declares that Jesus was despised and rejected of men, a man of sorrow, acquainted with grief. Jesus did not live a life of ecstasy, testifying every day of the wonders of God and the benefits. Instead, He was frequently grieved because of the ministry to which He was called. Jesus was not allowed to partake of this world's riches and desires, and although He was tempted on every side He was without sin.

REIGNING WITH CHRIST

In order to reign with Christ we must resign ourselves to the fact that we must also suffer with Him. The Bible tells us to rejoice when we are persecuted for Christ's sake. We can do this? We can do it as long as it is someone at work or someone at church or someone we have a business venture with. But can we do it when it is the one in whom we placed so much love, the one whom we became humiliated for? When the one persecuting us, the one who is denying us publicly, is he or she with whom we shared everything? What do you do when the one you have married has betrayed you?

Let's look at Jesus's example. His Word declares that He is married to the backslider. We read the parable of the two sons: one who was committed in all works to his father, the other who wanted to see the world and requested his inheritance early in order to do so. The father granted the request of the son who wanted to see the world, and into the world he went. After squandering all of his inheritance and finding out the true nature of people, he humbly returned home. His father received him with such love that it angered the other son. The father explained to the son who remained with him that he had been with him, had enjoyed the blessings of being in the house, but the son who was gone has returned, and as such would be restored to the place where he was before he left. It was the forgiveness of the father in the face of the betrayal of the son that developed the fruit of humility in the son, making him of greater stature than before he left. It appears that the glory of God is revealed in the life of the betrayer after he has been forgiven. Paul was a great religious man in the eyes of the world, but he was a betrayer of God. However, after this betrayal was revealed and God forgave him, he was greater after the betrayal than before it.

How can we know the forgiving power of Jesus unless He has made us aware of the fact that we have betrayed Him and, in spite of the facts, has offered to us forgiveness? It is when we forgive those who have betrayed us that they are set free to accomplish the mission of God in their life. It is in our forgiveness that they see Jesus in us.

Chapter 14

THE BATTLE IS NOT YOURS.
IT'S THE LORD'S.

Y OU ARE DEFINITELY in a battle, but whose battle is it? The Bible declares that King David was a man after God's own heart. When studying the life of David, the Scriptures tell us that as a young boy David had complete and total trust in the Lord. David defeated a lion and a bear with his own hands through the strength and power of God. David had the trust of a child and the wisdom to understand that he could do all things through God (Christ) who strengthens him. He never took any credit for his victories but continually stated that the Lord would deliver his enemies into his hands.

When we look at the passage of Scripture that tells us that David was a man after God's own heart, we interpret this saying as "a man dearly loved by God," which he in fact was. But that is not the true meaning of this phrase. David was a man who aggressively, continuously, consistently sought out the heart or will of God. David lived to please God and to be pleasing in His sight. He was a man who sought after, chased after God's own heart. Many of us, after we have gone through trial after trial only to look forward to the next one with no lasting relief, begin to lose trust in this God we so dearly want to please.

> And David said in his heart, I shall now perish one day by the hand of Saul: there is nothing better for me than that I should speedily escape into the land of the Philistines; and Saul shall despair of me, to seek me any more in any coast of Israel: so shall I escape out of his hand.
>
> —1 SAMUEL 27:1

When David took matters into his own hands and went to live in the enemy's camp, thereby dishonoring God, David would soon learn his helplessness and turn back to God, remembering who had been delivering him all along. David knew that he did not have the right from nor the approval of God to repay his enemies. God saw David as a righteous man because David lived his life to honor God. When David fought, it was on behalf of God, for God's people, under the direct command and orders of God. David never fought on behalf of himself but cried out to God for help in his time of trouble.

There you have it, the Psalms of David. Every psalm was a testimony of the goodness of God toward David, a recount of the many times that God had delivered him out of the hands of his enemies and a confession of his constant fear for his life. We also see David's cries of brokenness when confronted with his sin against God and his praise, worship, and continual adoration for the faithfulness and righteousness of the one true King, Jehovah. At no point did David put trust in himself, his soldiers, or his authority. David always humbly consulted with and submitted to the instruction and direction of the Lord.

THE PROTECTION OF OBEDIENCE

When God removed the anointing from Saul, David still regarded Saul as God's anointed and refused to harm him, thus committing a sin against God. David understood that who God had exalted, man could not demean nor dethrone. The same man whom God raises, God will bring down, but it is God who does both, not man.

Another example is when the man Nabal, whom David wanted to destroy because of his refusal to bless the men who had protected him, was saved from the wrath of David by the humility of his wife, Abigail. David was grateful to this woman, Abigail, because in her wisdom in coming to David she prevented David from doing what he had never done before, sin against God by handling God's business. In gratitude to this woman, David announced:

> And David said to Abigail, Blessed be the Lord God of Israel, which sent thee this day to meet me: And blessed be thy advice, and blessed be thou, which hast kept me this day from coming to shed blood, and from avenging myself with mine own hand. For in very deed, as the Lord God of Israel liveth, which hath kept me back from hurting thee, except thou hadst hasted and come to meet me, surely there had not been left unto Nabal by the morning light any that pisseth against the wall.
>
> —1 SAMUEL 25:32–34, 37–39

David, a man who lived to please the Lord, was our great example of God's favor upon those who will walk upright before him. David was not a perfect man, nor was David a man without sin. David was a man who knew explicitly his human frailties and placed no trust in himself. The Bible states that man looks at the outer appearance, but God looks at the heart. God was not moved by the appearances of the other sons of Jesse but had interest only in his youngest son, David. God considered this young lad to be wise when others saw him merely as a shepherd boy because God knew that David's trust was not in his own ability but in the Lord's.

PRIDE OR RIGHTEOUSNESS

Consider the statement that says, "I cannot because I am not capable or worthy." It is a statement of pride in the sight of God, because it means that we place confidence in our own ability. David, on the other hand, uses the statement, "I can because my Lord will do it through me." This is a righteous man before God, one who is capable of conquering any battle.

The sword of the spirit is the Word of God. The Word of the Lord is powerful and sharper than any two-edged sword. The Word, or the sword, does the slaying, not the one who holds the sword (the Word). The Word, which is God's very voice, His heart, and His intention, never needs validating by human efforts. The All-Powerful need only be obeyed in His instruction, for it pleases God to honor us by performing His good pleasure through us.

We must know and understand emphatically that God does not need us to accomplish His will. He desires to bless and has purposed in His heart, out of the love for us, to bless us. We have been counted worthy to suffer (to battle, to endure trials and tribulation) for the Lord's sake; this is a great honor. David did not see fighting Goliath as a punishment from God. He did not ask, "Why me?" as if some terrible thing were happening to him, but he counted it an honor to be chosen by God to war on behalf of God, knowing without a doubt that God was with him and he would be victorious. David did not consider defeat, because he knew that his God could not be defeated.

WE GLORY IN TRIBULATION

We whine and cry over our trials and tribulations as if God has rejected us or is punishing us in some way when in fact the opposite is true. In allowing us to be warriors, God is in fact blessing us. He has chosen by His grace and for His own good pleasure to anoint us and extend His favor toward us. In Old Testament times, being chosen as a warrior in the king's army was an honor. Men gladly died for their country, for their king, and for their family. We, on the other hand, cry to be delivered from the very thing that brings honor to our King of kings and Lord of lords. We must, as David did, be driven by the desire to obtain the heart of God, to be favored by our Lord.

A man who is pleasing in the sight of God is the one who places absolute trust in God. In this we find a righteous man, a man after God's own heart.

Chapter 15

THE WORD OF GOD
SPOKEN, MADE FLESH

IT WAS THE spoken, prophetic utterance of Joseph concerning his own life that was placed in Joseph by God,
and it was that word or will of God in Joseph's life that
had to be tested. It is not us that the devil tempts and God
tests, but it is God's own words and God's own nature in
us that is being tested. The spoken will of God sets it all in
motion (the testing and the tempting). Nothing can happen,
good or bad, without God speaking it. It does not exist unless
and until He speaks it.

> All things were made by him; and without him was not
> any thing made that was made.
>
> —JOHN 1:3

Everything created was spoken by God. Everything re-created was re-created by the creation of God. Nothing exists in
and of itself, and nothing returns to nothing. All that was
created is created, and all that ever was still is, and all that
exists came forth out of the mouth of God.

UNDERSTANDING AUTHORITY

> And when Jesus was entered into Capernaum, there
> came unto him a centurion, beseeching him, And
> saying, Lord, my servant lieth at home sick of the palsy,

grievously tormented. And Jesus saith unto him, I will come and heal him. The centurion answered and said, Lord, I am not worthy that thou shouldest come under my roof: but speak the word only, and my servant shall be healed. For I am a man under authority, having soldiers under me: and I say to this man, Go, and he goeth; and to another, Come, and he cometh; and to my servant, Do this, and he doeth it. When Jesus heard it, he marvelled, and said to them that followed, Verily I say unto you, I have not found so great faith, no, not in Israel....And Jesus said unto the centurion, Go thy way; and as thou hast believed, so be it done unto thee. And his servant was healed in the selfsame hour.

—MATTHEW 8:5–10, 13

The thing we must understand is it was not until the apostle Paul came on the scene that the gospel began to be preached to the Gentiles. Up to that time, Jesus's ministry was primarily to the Jews. Periodically Jesus would come across someone who was not a Jew and would have mercy on him or her and heal and deliver, but these examples were few and far between. First of all, this centurion was not "one of the children of Israel," had not been raised up in the Law, and was not familiar with the oracles and commands, as were the Jewish believers; yet, he understood authority. What is marvelous in this passage is that although he understood authority, it was by faith that he believed that Jesus was One who possessed authority. The soldier had no problem with the understanding of authority, because he was under authority to some and had authority over others. He understood the commands and the power of the Commander. Therefore, knowing Jesus was the Son of God, someone in high authority, he also knew that Jesus must have someone under Him.

A person is not in leadership and does not have authority

over nothing. There must be something or someone whom they command. In this centurion's mind, he knew that Jesus not only had authority, but he understood what and whom He had authority over. He knew that Jesus had authority over sickness and disease, which means he understood infallibly that Jesus was the Son of God. Once you believe without question that Jesus is the Son of God, you *must* then know that *all* things are possible for Him to accomplish.

Jesus continued in His response, stating that the great religious people would be cast into the lake, but the so-called "no-names" would sit with Him in His kingdom. Faith in Jesus is more valuable than any religious order or following and is greater than any earthly command.

SATAN'S TEMPTATION OF CHRIST

When the devil tempted Jesus, it was not the human he was trying to destroy; it was everything that God had said about this Christ that was the target. Remember, when speaking with Eve the devil said to her, "Did God say...?" Satan couldn't care less about Eve. It was God's Word—the substance all creation and the substance of all that had been created—that the devil was opposing.

No one knows better than Satan the power of the Word of the Lord. No one knows better the character of God and how He must remain true to His word. So, Satan attempts to get God to go against His Word by His love for us. The Bible declares that God is love. The Bible also says that heaven and earth will pass away, but God's Word would remain forever. So, the two most important aspects of the nature of God— His love and His Word—have been the target of Satan from Adam and Eve to the close of Revelation. His desire is to get one tittle of God's Word to fail. If Satan can get one aspect of God's Word to fail, then all of it, including God Himself, fails. This is why God is compelled to deal with sin. God, who is holy, can in no uncertain terms tolerate or excuse sin. Sin must be dealt with. So there we have it, our precious Savior taking on the penalty of the sins of the world. Only Jesus, a sinless God manifested in the flesh, was qualified to take away our sins.

Joseph's Spoken Word

> And Joseph dreamed a dream, and he told it his brethren: and they hated him yet the more. And he said unto them, Hear, I pray you, this dream which I have dreamed: For, behold, we were binding sheaves in the field, and, lo, my sheaf arose, and also stood upright; and, behold, your sheaves stood round about, and made obeisance to my sheaf. And his brethren said to him, Shalt thou indeed reign over us? or shalt thou indeed have dominion over us? And they hated him yet the more for his dreams, and for his words. And he dreamed yet another dream, and told it his brethren, and said, Behold, I have dreamed a dream more; and, behold, the sun and the moon and the eleven stars made obeisance to me.... And they took Joseph's coat, and killed a kid of the goats, and dipped the coat in the blood; And they sent the coat of many colours, and they brought it to their father; and said, This have we found: know now whether it be thy son's coat or no.
>
> —Genesis 37: 5–9, 31–32

Once Joseph spoke the will of God over his life, all hell broke loose. God began the process of testing, and Satan (by permission) began the processing of tempting. God was testing Joseph to ensure faithfulness to Him once He brought Him into his kingdom, and Satan was tempting Joseph with evil from his brothers to sin against God by hating and having bitterness toward them. Notice how God and Satan are using the same circumstance, but how we respond in the circumstance determines who our ruler ultimately becomes.

We must understand that God's Word spoken over our life is yea and amen, but it will always have to be proven. God's Word must refine us so that we spring forth as pure gold.

If I render myself dead to sin, redeemed by Jesus, then there is no evil in me. There is no iniquity, there is no battle, and there is no fight. Everything from the point of salvation and redemption on has *nothing to do with me*! God spoke it, and it is so. I agree with God, and I experience the manifestation of that spoken Word in my life. I glory in the reality that I have been deemed worthy to suffer for and with Christ so that I may reign with Him. What an honor it is to be persecuted for Christ's sake.

Chapter 16

BACK TO THE GARDEN

I<small>N THE BEGINNING</small> God created man in His image and in His likeness. Sin defiled the likeness of God in man, but Jesus's death and resurrection gave it back to us. Unfortunately, because of our sinful nature and the length of time for which we carried this nature, getting the lie out of us is also a lengthy process. Add to that having to put the truth back into us, and there we have yet another lengthy process. It is important to understand that truth cannot be imputed to us until the lie has been purged out of us. It is not until the lie is exposed by the continuous destruction of it that we even accept it as such.

OUR SIN NATURE

The sin nature fortifies our sinful bodies, and vice versa. While the earth produces nourishment (bread) needed for our bodies, it does not satisfy the sinful man. Man desires "processed" food developed by the sin nature of man, which produces death in the body, rather than fruit produced by a sinless God, which provides life to the body. Why is it that our flesh yearns for the sinful nature? I believe that we found pleasure though our sin nature and feel as if we're missing out on something in giving it up. While the repercussions to our sin were horrendous, the momentary pleasure from the sin seems to play like a tape recorder in our minds. Our old nature is protected, almost as if put on a shelf to refer back to in case "this God thing" doesn't work out the way we want.

There it is, the heart of the problem: not only do we want to control ourselves, but our evil nature and our evil heart literally wants to control God. We want to manipulate God into our desires by surrendering only a portion of ourselves, not realizing that the Creator of the heart knows the intent of the heart and the evil therein. We offer sacrifices to God, sacrifices that we have deemed acceptable to Him, and in our pride and arrogance we are offended when God does not accept them. The Bible declares that the sacrifices of God are a broken spirit and a contrite heart (a heart overcome by grief and despair, a heart that is repentant, has a feeling of sorrow for sins or offenses). Only this person will be sorry enough to surrender his or her will to God. It is not enough just to tell God that we are sorry. If we are really sorry, we will surrender wholly to God.

OUR DESTRUCTIVE NATURE

Our nature craves, desires, and continuously requests destructive things. Although the redemptive work of Christ on the cross was for the purpose of reconciling us back to our Father, we still were without a desire for Him. The Bible declares that no man can come to Christ unless He draws him. Simply put, in and of ourselves we do not have a desire to know Christ. It is in the simplicity of the gospel, in unwavering acceptance of the redemptive work of Christ on the cross without knowing the details that the process of changing our nature can begin. While we cannot explain why we came to Christ, we do know that there was this pull, and the Word of God spoken to us made inexplicable sense.

What is happening here is that God decided of His own

accord, for His own reasons, that He wanted to reveal Himself to us. God decided that He wanted to work in and through us His good pleasure. Once we are chosen by God, He begins the process of reversing the lie told to us by Satan and taught to us by our parents, who before us were told the same lie. I grew up believing that love was destructive and therefore protected myself against it at all cost! I believed that the only safety net I had was the one that I produced; depend on no one, trust no one, and strive to obtain financial security for yourself and your family. Intimacy was restricted to the physical, and emotional connections brought on unnecessary complications. I based my life on lies: "I am not the head, but the tail. I am not the above only; I am the beneath. Prosperity is for someone else, and holiness is for the monk. Ministry is for the educated, and I deserved the abuse I received as payment for sin. Jesus did not pay the entire price, as I have my portion to pay. I will never be clean. I remain defiled." And the biggest lie of all: "God is a God of love, and therefore *all* sin will be excused, because God understands our weaknesses and will pardon my willful, uncontrollable rebellion."

ADAM AND EVE

Adam and Eve found out the hard way that there is most definitely a repercussion to sin. As Paul wrote, "Shall we continue in sin, that grace may abound? God forbid!" (Rom. 6:1–2). The greatest sin is the sin of pride. Pride leads to the total and complete destruction of a man, because it allows for deception to reign within him. It is a lie that causes man to be deceived, and it is pride that causes a man to continue in the deception that ultimately leads to rebellion.

While we do sin because we have a sin nature, it is important to note that in the case of Adam and Eve, there was no sin nature. It wasn't their nature that drew them into sin. It was, in fact, pride. Pride caused Adam and Eve to sin against God. You see, Adam and Eve were created totally dependent upon God. They knew no other way. In this dependent state the glory of God was their garment. They were in complete harmony with the earth and lived glorious lives, lives that we cannot even fathom. What more could they want?

Many theologians argue that they wanted to be like God or like gods. I submit to you that they didn't necessarily want to be God; they wanted the ability to think and act independently of God, to find out the secret to this forbidden tree. Although God told them everything there was to know about this tree, informed them that their eyes would be open and that they would know good from evil, they still wanted the "experience." I can remember at age seventeen my biological father sitting down with me and discussing life and some of its pitfalls. After he finished, I vividly remember saying to him, "Daddy, you can talk to me all you want, but until I actually experience it, it doesn't mean anything to me." Although Daddy warned me, it was my pride that insisted on having the experience that brought a lifetime of heartache and pain to me. How often as we provide all the necessities for our children do they respond to us as if there is something that we're holding back from them and determine to find out what that something is? Yet, in our wisdom we are simply trying to protect them from having to experience unnecessary pain and disappointment.

GETTING RID OF THE PRIDE

The center of all sin is pride. In its best definition, it is the prideful individual who shifts ultimate confidence from God to self. Now, in order to find out who I was before the life of pride, it is needful for me to look at my original state. The first step in returning to this original state is accepting Jesus's atoning blood for my sins and willfully giving back the control of my life to Him. Next, allow the Holy Spirit to purge out and undo my earthly training. Everything I learned now must be unlearned—my thought patterns, my eating habits, my communication skills, my problem-solving techniques, and so on. The problem in accomplishing this is that my pride has convinced me that my ways are right. I find myself thinking like Paul after his conversion, "Lord, you mean everything I learned is wrong? Wow! OK, I accept that. But now how in the world do I unlearn it?"

THE HOLY SPIRIT

The Holy Spirit begins the process of purging our sinful nature, but not without a tremendous fight. If I give up my anger, my greed, my lustful nature, then I'll be vulnerable, vulnerable to this God I know nothing of and vulnerable to the people around me. You see, Adam and Eve knew God and yet still chose to rebel against him. "But God, I am expected to give up everything I know for a God I don't know?" Jesus gave us the precious gift of the Holy Spirit, who not only purges us from embedded sin but also reveals Jesus to us, who in turn reveals the Father. Now as we begin to learn about our Savior, who was God incarnate, and simultaneously learn of our Father God, our desire to know Him increases, and our desire to obey Him deepens.

Remember, Adam and Eve were totally dependent upon God. They were, in the greatest definition, humble. They began as humble creatures, and through the sin of pride became rebellious. God wants to return us to our original state of humility from our current rebellious state. God wants to return us back to the future!

Who was I before the lie? I was a loving, joyous, peaceful, long-suffering, gentle, good, faithful, meek, and self-controlled person. Pride—and the rebellion of it—produces adultery, fornication, idol worship, witchcraft, hatred, troublemaking, jealousy, anger, selfishness, strife divisions, envy, drunkenness, and wild living.

Jesus, our Perfect Example

The Bible lets us know that while Jesus was being beaten and tortured, He endured as a sheep lead away to the slaughter, in complete humility. We read in Isaiah 53:7, "He opened not his mouth." If the Son of the God of the universe, if God Incarnate, opened not His mouth in suffering, then what right do we have to question God? Jesus, the Son of God, made a humble request to God with a broken heart and a contrite spirit in the Garden of Gethsemane, yet we make demands to God of things that are not even His will without having properly obtained His ear. What arrogance!

Entering God's presence without a sacrifice is an abomination. The sacrifice acceptable to God was the blood of Jesus Christ. Only an individual with a broken heart and a contrite spirit will seek cleansing through the blood of Jesus for the washing away of his or her sins. We cannot request the redemptive work of Christ for ourselves without first presenting a broken heart and a contrite spirit. This is the way many approach God, and they have an emotional experience but walk away and immediately experience the same battle and conflicts. If this happens, we did not approach God with an acceptable sacrifice and therefore were not able to receive deliverance and cleansing by Jesus's blood. We have confused emotional sensations with a touch from God. When God cleanses an area, it is clean, and there is no residue left. When we sincerely desire to be rid of a sin, we will do it God's way.

We have a sin nature, and as such, our flesh desires to be in control rather than yielding control to God. If giving up an area of our life to God for cleansing and deliverance in some way strips us of the deceptive power we believe we have, then we will reject cleaning in that area. In other words, "If it's going to leave me vulnerable, then I don't want it!" The enemy has taught us and reiterated to us that God gave us our personality, and it is needful to fight against those who would attempt to hurt us to protect ourselves. Although the Bible tells us as Christians that the battle is not ours but the Lord's, the enemy would have us to believe that God empowered us and expects us to use this power to fight back. Again, the distortion is to take control rather than give control to God. It is an ongoing battle against sin and pride that causes the circle of frustration in our lives.

The Holy Tabernacle

After the blood of Jesus Christ has cleansed us, we give thanks for His mercies, which are new every morning. We are now at the gate. But that is not enough. We began to think about His goodness and mercy and the fact that He sent His only Son to be a ransom for us. We want to get closer to Him, so we enter into the outer court. We began to feel His glory, and His presence is like a vacuum, which sucks us in until we find ourselves in the inner court. We are transformed into the image of God's Son, Jesus. God would ask us, "How much do you want me? How much do you love me? Are you willing to say good-bye to yourself, to press past your fleshly desires, your dreams, goals, and ambitions? Are you willing to be cleansed completely with no residue of your fleshly desires? Are you willing to press past the gates, past the outer courts, and enter into the inner courts to be transformed?"

Who was I before the lie? I was totally dependent upon God, and as a result I knew only the goodness, protection, and providence of God. I knew no lack, I knew no pain, and I knew no sorrow—only joy unspeakable and full of glory. Who was I before the lie? I was a son.

Chapter 17

THE PROCESS OF THE CALL

*For he shall give his angels charge over thee, to keep
thee in all thy ways. They shall bear thee up in their
hands, lest thou dash thy foot against a stone.*

—PSALM 91:11–12

T HE PROCESS OF God testing us in our lives may be likened to the actions of the eagle. I heard Joyce Meyer teach on the eagle, and in her twenty-minute television session, she spoke about how the female eagle tests the male eagle. The portion of the message I heard described how the female eagle would take a twig and drop it, causing the male eagle to dive for it. At each stage of her testing, she would take a heavier twig and drop it from a lower altitude, making it more difficult for the male eagle each time. Joyce did not get into the continuation of this message on this particular segment, and I was unable to get her teaching tapes, but by the prompting of the Holy Spirit the Lord has given me some insight into exactly what is happening here. The female eagle is testing the male eagle to see if he is not only worthy to father her offspring but trustworthy to care for them, to ensure that he would be able to prevent them from dashing their foot against the stone. Would he be aggressive enough, keen enough, and caring enough to protect her young?

God in His infinite wisdom is likened unto the mother eagle. Later this same God is seen as the father eagle. God chooses who will father His offspring. In the case of Abraham, God declared that Abraham would be the father of many nations, and the number of Abraham's offspring would be compared to the sand. The Messiah would come through him, yet this prospective father of many nations must first be tested.

THE PROMISE

God had given Abraham a promise, a promise that would not be fulfilled for many years. There were many reasons to doubt this promise, including the fact that the wife who would bear the promise was barren. After failing to trust in the promise of God and the resulting manifestation of that doubt, which produced Ishmael, the promise was ultimately fulfilled. God, as the mother in this case, will not only choose a mate to bring forth her seed, but will test this mate before using him. After God has chosen us to birth forth His promises and His will through us, He then becomes the Father, the One who teaches, guides, protects, and instructs us in His ways so that we will be as He is.

> As an eagle stirreth up her nest, fluttereth over her young, spreadeth abroad her wings, taketh them, beareth them on her wings: So the Lord alone did lead him, and there was no strange god with him.
>
> —DEUTERONOMY 32:11–12

Can you be trusted? God first determines whether or not we can be trusted. There are people who are dedicated, trusted workers. They have been on their jobs for twenty-five years and can be totally trusted with the safe deposit key. However, the man committed to the work is not necessarily committed to God. We see this in the case of Paul (Saul), who was totally committed, even unto death, to the religious traditions of his day but was in fact not at all committed to God. God must establish and test our commitment to Him before He joins Himself with us to accomplish His plan through us, to place His seed in us.

OUR TRAINING

Once born, eaglets are stirred up in the nest. It is now time for their training. Likewise, God must stir us up. God will train the one whom He has chosen to bear Him fruit. Later, the one who has been chosen by God must bear more fruit. This chosen one must also prove himself worthy to be able to protect the fruit that God will allow him to bear.

God places a call on our lives and imputes a desire to carry out that call. In God's protectiveness, He broods over us. In His protectiveness, He basically does everything for us. He foresees dangers approaching us and wards them off without our ever knowing the danger existed. There is a blind trust in God's provision, and He is our great Protector. As we mature, God begins to train us in His ways.

Although we are born in His image and likeness, because of sin we are tempted to live by the dictates of our flesh; therefore, God must begin to empower and teach us how to live as we should, in the spirit. The eagles do not teach the eaglet how to live like a chicken; neither are horses taught to live like pigs. The eagle teaches its eaglets how to be eagles. We are the children of God, made in His image. We must be taught how to be like our Father. The ministry of Christ was for the exact purpose of showing us God on a human level. Jesus said that when we had seen Him, we had seen the Father. Jesus gave us many examples of the kingdom of God. However, it was through and by His person that He showed us the person of God. It was by example. So it is with the eagle.

Deuteronomy 32:11–12 was given by inspiration before the Savior was born. There were many attempts by God to help man to understand Him and His relationship to them. Of course, the ultimate revelation was His Incarnate Son. For now, however, we will deal with the revelation by the example from the eagle. The eagle spreads out his wings, and with the eaglets on his wings, begins to take them into the air. He takes them up and then drops them. Knowing that they cannot yet protect themselves but knowing still that they must be acquainted with this process, he does it anyway. The eagle descends at a rate of two hundred miles per hour, catching the eaglets before "they dash their foot against the stone" (Ps. 91:12). The eagle does this over and over again until the eaglets learn to fly themselves.

GOD'S ULTIMATE PLAN

While we are in training God doesn't just drop us into the circumstances, the trials, and tribulations of life without a plan to catch us. We enter into circumstances on the "wings" of God. His presence encamps around us to protect us against being consumed while in training. Not only do we begin to learn by example, but God also periodically tests us to see how far we have progressed. There will most assuredly come a day when, like the eaglet, we are dropped and ultimately learn to fly on our own. As the process repeats itself, we eventually learn to soar and are dispatched as disciples. We not only become teachers and disciples, but we are now well equipped to train up our own seed.

Chapter 18

STRATEGIC POSITIONING

POSITION IS A place occupied by a person or object in relation to another person or object. Position can also be described as a "maneuver" for position. Like a chess game, all moves are strategic, well thought out and planned, arranged precisely by the Master for the purpose of defeating the opponent. While the chess pieces represent ranks and status, it is the Master who designates the spaces and positions those pieces occupy. It is the Master's primary goal to defeat the opponent and conquer His king; however, it was needful for the position and status of the pieces to be established before the game began.

A PLAN TO CONQUER

God in His infinite wisdom not only promised to crush the enemy's head but to totally and completely humiliate him by releasing sinful flesh from his control and empowering us to continually overcome him in the flesh. In addition, God has equipped these redeemed sinners to go into the enemy's camp and destroy his plans.

> For this purpose the Son of God was manifested, that he might destroy the works of the devil.
>
> —1 JOHN 3:8

Because God is precise and does not shoot at the dark, God has given His people individually as well as corporately a specific ground to conquer. Much work must be done to properly train these chosen warriors. They must develop senses in which they have not beforehand known or used. They must be turned from their disobedient ways and learn total and complete obedience and surrender to their Master, because the slightest move to the left or the right, a misunderstanding, could not only cause their destruction but cause the whole plan to be aborted.

Positioning requires patience, careful thought, delicacy, and skill. One must have studied and be knowledgeable of the enemy. We do not know the mind or the heart of Satan. Only God, his Creator, knows the degree of the evil within him, and only God, his Creator, knows his intent. Therefore, it is only God who can direct us in our war against him.

THE WEAPONS OF OUR WARFARE ARE NOT CARNAL

It is important to remember that as children of the King, we are protected by our Master. We have the right to the use of the armor that protects us from all the fiery darts of the wicked one. However, we are very much in a war on behalf of those who have not come into a saving knowledge of our Lord and Savior Jesus Christ. Jesus Himself said that He did not come for those who were not in need of a physician; He came to heal the brokenhearted, to heal the sick, to bring deliverance to the captives, to preach the acceptable year of the Lord. Our job is to proclaim that Jesus did exactly that and, to prove it, use the power that His resurrection gave to us, the power through the Holy Ghost. We should be laying hands on the sick and seeing them recover, restoring sight to the blind, healing the brokenhearted, and casting out devils.

We are to wage war against the dark forces of the enemy on behalf of those who are bound. If in war, my goal is to get into the wicked king's palace and release the prisoners held there. If I zealously burst through the doors without having obtained instruction on how many guards are in the outer courts or how many are in the inner courts or where exactly the prisoners are kept, then the moment I burst through those doors immediately I face an onslaught of attack and am defeated. If lucky, I escape with my life. However, I am now wounded, humiliated, frustrated, and discouraged. If I die, I am not even a hero. Then what good were my good heart, my good intentions, and my zealousness?

WE NEED A VISION

Without a vision, the people perish. Without a course, I become a wanderer. Without instruction, I become blind. Without a master, I exist alone. Abiding alone, I can do nothing.

Who has desired to please God in and of himself besides Christ? Who has chosen this course for Christ? No one. It is God who has chosen us and, through His mercy, has implanted within us a desire to please Him. That same God who implanted the desire does not now turn over the working-out of that desire to us! He must begin to work out in us the desire *He* placed within us. Oftentimes for encouragement God shows us glimpses of the work to which He has called us, and in our prematurity we aggressively strive to accomplish the vision that God has for us. A perfect example of this was seen in the apostle Peter. Jesus told Peter that He would build His church upon the rock of the knowledge of

Jesus Christ that Peter professed and that the gates of hell would not prevail against it. Peter knew that he was favored by Jesus and that he would do great exploits through Him; however, through much pain and disappointment Peter found out that this greatness would have to be worked out in him over a period of time and after much suffering.

GOD'S LEADING

The word premature is, simply stated, pre-mature, meaning "before maturity." It is the state before we mature. To go forth in ministry or in the operation of our call before we have matured in God would be likened to a woman travailing in birth before her time. She may produce a very sickly baby, or the baby may die. Our ministries are sickly because they were born prematurely. Some of our visions have died due to premature births. As individuals, we have become frustrated, dull, defeated, and depressed because we have gone into a life requiring maturity before we have matured.

> For it is God which worketh in you both to will and to do of his good pleasure.
>
> —PHILIPPIANS 2:13

> In whom also we have obtained an inheritance, being predestinated according to the purpose of him who worketh all things after the counsel of his own will.
>
> —EPHESIANS 1:11

We have been predestined to the purpose of God. And if God, who predestines all of His creation, has mapped out our life before we were born, how do we then change its course? Who can change the heart of God, His direction, or His plan?

Who can take counsel with Him? Can the creation say to its Creator, make me this way or give me that?

Webster's Dictionary describes *predestination* this way: "the doctrine that everything was determined by God from the beginning, esp. with reference to the play of divine omnipotence and human freewill in determining the fate of the soul." What is quite interesting in this definition is the word *play*. Another definition of the word *play* in its context might be "competition." The competition between God's omnipotence in predestination and our will not only serves to prove to us that God's will always prevails, but through our defeat to God we surrender our own attempts to control ourselves and submit our will to Him. It is at this point that God, the controller of our hearts, transforms these stony hearts into hearts that please Him.

There is not only a battle after the surrender, but it is a battle that causes the surrender. It is after we have attempted to control our own lives and failed that we come to a realization that we cannot.

Now, after coming to the realization we could not live a life pleasing to God without Him, we come to Him. We now believe we can do all things through Christ who strengthens us and attempt to go forth only in our own ability, with Christ as our backup. There we go, back on the Potter's wheel until we get to the realization that our natural ability can never please God. However, even while we are doing our own thing, God is still strategically orchestrating our every move.

Chapter 19

HIS POWER

IT IS NOT for me to use His power, but rather it is His power that uses me. We are under the impression that Jesus has given us His power and determined over time, through tests and trials, that God has deemed us fit to receive His power, along with discretion and authority over the use of this power. We have rejected the prayers of the apostles, wherein Peter prayed after being released from prison that God would empower them to do greater works for Him with boldness.

> And now, Lord, behold their threatenings: and grant unto thy servants, that with all boldness they may speak thy word, By stretching forth thine hand to heal; and that signs and wonders may be done by the name of thy holy child Jesus. And when they had prayed, the place was shaken where they were assembled together; and they were all filled with the Holy Ghost, and they spake the word of God with boldness.
>
> —ACTS 4:29–31

This prayer came after they had been in the Upper Room, had received the impartation of the Holy Ghost, and had already gone forth in power, healing the lame man and winning many souls to the Lord. If Peter, having walked with Jesus, being tried and tested and afterward being called an apostle, still needed to pray and ask Jesus to permit them to speak and do signs and wonders in His name, how much more ought we to ask permission of Jesus to use His power and authority?

POWER THROUGH SUBMISSION

We know Jesus as a Savior, we know Him as the Son of God, we know Him as the crucified Savior, but we don't know Him as King of kings and Lord of lords. Americans have very little to no understanding of royalty and the respect that's due one in this position.

What is a king? One who rules and reigns for life. Over the centuries, there were many kings, but as ambassadors for God, many of them failed in their attempts to rule according to the strict ordinances of God. Jesus, the King of all kings, was not only totally submitted to the command of God, but totally committed to the people over which He ruled. Jesus earned His position as King of kings and Lord of lords, as well as High Priest. The Bible declares that although He was yet a son, Christ learned obedience by the things which He suffered (Heb. 5:8). Jesus as a sacrificial Lamb obeyed His Master, His Father, even to the point of death. He did not assume His role as King but took on Himself the form of a servant who was later exalted by God.

Jesus, as God's Son, did only what God instructed Him to do. He did not add to, neither did He take away from, the plan and purpose of God. Jesus did not assume the rights and privileges but made His petitions to the Father through prayer. If Jesus, God in the flesh, the Son of God, the Anointed One, needed to ask permission from God to use the power that God gave Him, how much more do we need permission to use the power given us? It is not the power in us under our direction, but it is the Jesus in us, prompting our person for His desire and for His purpose.

We are but vessels of clay. We breathe by the assistance and the command of God. Without him, we can do nothing. If we cannot command this clay to speak, walk, stand without the assistance of God, how can we command spiritual activities without the assistance or command of God?

Our bodies are the "temple" of God. They make up His residence. This residence is located within the person of Christ— He in us, and we in Him. He has placed in us everything He needs in order to do whatever He wants to do, whenever He wants or needs to do it. His will is activated by the Holy Spirit within us. God has also placed His Word in us so that whenever a situation arises where Jesus needs His Word to be activated to accomplish a specific goal surrounding this particular temple, He quickens and/or uses what has already been placed in the temple.

Some Christians do not have a call from the Lord, but then there are those who have not only been called but have been chosen by God to show the extent of man's evil, even in the face of God Almighty. These are those possessing the spirit of the Antichrist (an opponent of the Messiah). They claim to worship in the name of Jesus, they seem to lay hands on the sick in the name of Jesus, they appear to teach the Word of God, but they are enemies of God. Like Judas, they betray Jesus with a kiss.

> Many will say to me in that day, Lord, Lord, have we not prophesied in thy name? and in thy name have cast out devils? and in thy name done many wonderful works? And then will I profess unto them, I never knew you: depart from me, ye that work iniquity.
>
> —MATTHEW 7:22–23

Chapter 20

AUTHORITY TO USE HIS POWER

THE NAME OF Jesus carries with it power. The name of Jesus, the person of Jesus, the deity of Jesus, the God in Jesus does not need man's faith in Jesus in order for the power of Jesus and His name to be validated. The Word declares that Jesus could not do many miracles in His own town because of the unbelief of the people. However, there are several other accounts when Jesus healed or delivered (as in the possessed man in the tombs) without getting permission or agreement from the individual.

Jesus and His Spirit (the Holy Spirit) search and know the heart of man. Jesus hears what the man cannot speak. He knows the evil intents of a person appearing innocent, and He knows the pure intents of a person appearing evil. Jesus could do few miracles in His own country because the people were seeking Jesus to prove Himself, especially since these were people who knew of His heritage; knew His family; had seen Him in the light of a boy, a teenager, and a young man who by all appearances was no different from them. It is important to reiterate that man's unbelief does not limit God's decision to move on their behalf. It is the impurity of the heart, which God sees, that determines Jesus's (the Holy Spirit's) decision to move on behalf of that person.

Jesus told the disciples that they would do greater works because He was going to the Father. As stated earlier, the name of Jesus (all by itself) carries with it immeasurable power; however, Jesus let His disciples know that there would be greater power to accompany His name after He sent the Comforter (the Holy Spirit) to dwell within them.

THE INFILLING OF THE HOLY SPIRIT

Prior to the infilling of the Holy Spirit, the Spirit of God was outwardly assisting the disciples. And again, it was the use of the name of Jesus that quickened the Holy Spirit to assist the user of the name. After Pentecost, this power became resident in the believer; however, it is still intended to be used only at the direction and discretion of Jesus.

Our nation was founded on the precept of servanthood. The leaders of this country were put into position based on the idea that they would serve the people and dedicate their lives to ensuring that they performed those things they promised. We have seen through generations that oftentimes those men and women were, in fact, using their positions for personal gain, not for the benefit of the people (as promised).

So it is with false Christians. The name of Jesus carries with itself power, and everything on earth and under the earth is subject to that name. If God does not want a thing to be accomplished in a person, whether it is healing or deliverance, God must command the evil spirit to resist. Oftentimes, even though it is a wicked person using the name of Jesus, God will allow it because of the need of the individual seeking God, not for the benefit of the wicked person. In the Book of Acts, Peter, an apostle of Jesus Christ, filled with the Holy Spirit and called by God, an eyewitness to the accounts of Jesus, prayed and asked God to grant freedom to him to declare the message of Christ fearlessly. Why?

THE DISCIPLES' TRAINING

Peter understood that being called by God, being an eye-witness to the miracles of Jesus, being present at His death, eating with Jesus, living with Him, seeing Him, spending time with Him after the Resurrection, and being filled with His Spirit all meant one thing: that he was an "official servant." Peter understood that this all meant that Jesus owned Him, lock, stock, and barrel, and his life no longer belonged to him.

In the twentieth century, this concept of slavery, owner, master, and bond servant is foreign to many people in the United States, because we have been born and raised in a free country. We live in a nation of free choice. "If it feels good, do it." Even as employees, if we feel that we can rebel against a boss who pays us, how much more rebellious are we to someone who gives to us freely, without work? The disciples understood the precepts of master and servant. They knew that of all masters, Jesus was the great Master, the Master of all creation, One of highest esteem and deserving full reverence and sacrifice. Like good servants, they desired in the uttermost to please their Master.

Originally, in their early walk with Jesus, the disciples asked for power for personal gain. They even argued among themselves as to who the greatest of them was. They were looking for an earthly kingdom (a great church), so that they would be honored by the people. However, after the experience with Jesus, after coming to know the height, depth, and width of Jesus's love, the disciples' desires had changed. They did not ask for power for personal gain, but with all humility they sought to bring honor to the Great One.

Prior to Pentecost, the disciples were given the authority by Jesus to use His name as they followed Jesus and were taught by Him. However, after Jesus died and rose, they fervently desired His Spirit to live inside of them. They were no longer satisfied to be followers of Jesus in life; it was no longer enough just to see the name work, to be highly regarded by the people as an apostle of Christ. They wanted wholly to please this Jesus, to be in Him and Him in them—so much so that they did not leave the place in which they were worshiping (the Upper Room) until they received the "clothing" of the Holy Spirit. They would not again use His name until He had "endued" them, or filled them up, with His power, and it would only be by permission through humility for God's purpose.

That power not only equipped them to do the work of the ministry but gave them a true and deeper revelation and understanding of the Jesus whom they would serve. The Spirit of God in them testified of Jesus's deity by anointing the proclamation and reaffirming it through signs and wonders. It was necessary for the disciples not only to have the authority and power to use the name of Jesus, but to love wisdom and possess dedication to Christ and *His* will. Those people who will be told by Jesus to depart from Him are those who wanted the power of Jesus without the submission to Him. These are the ones who themselves wanted to be reverenced and praised and were considered by Jesus thieves and robbers. These are those who will hear Him say, "Depart from me, I never knew you. You used my name (a name of power) to make yourself look good before people, but you yourself did not even obey my words. My name worked in spite of you and had nothing to do with your person."

Chapter 21

OUR BODY, THE TEMPLE OF GOD

A S A RESULT of sin, man's spirit became independent of God and was subject to the mastery of Satan. Jesus restored man's ability to be joined with God, but now man must press through the sinful nature and choose his original master. Once the choice is made for God, the Holy Spirit rejoins and reconnects man to God. When that connection is made, we become conscious of the battle between the Spirit of the Lord (the Holy Spirit) and the spirit of Satan. My body is the temple of the Holy Spirit; therefore, my soul, or my mind, wills and desires to be enslaved by the Holy Spirit and willingly yields itself as a servant to the commands of the Lord.

My flesh, this temple of God, must at all costs bring honor to its Master, the Holy Spirit. Satan seeks to bring dishonor to the Holy Spirit by weakening my flesh or conscious defenses through worry, distrust, anger, unforgiveness, pride, rebellion, and physical fatigue. Once Satan has temporary control over my flesh through sin (or any of the above), he launches an all-out attack against my regenerated spirit for control of my soul. My new regenerated spirit must be chosen, asked, requested by me to fight on my behalf the spirit of darkness for the control of my soul. This is done through repentance (a decision to change, to return back to my master, Jesus). Once I have yielded my will or my soul to the leadership of Jesus, under the direction of the Holy Spirit, the war in my flesh on behalf of my soul is now between Jesus and Satan.

WHOSE BATTLE IS IT?

This life and these battles are not about us. They are about our risen Savior, our King of kings and Lord of lords. Satan hates everyone who names the name of Jesus. It is the Jesus in us that Satan desires to destroy. He not only wants to ultimately destroy us, but he wants to pervert the person of Jesus through us. But know this: Jesus has already defeated him. Because our spirit has been regenerated by the Holy Spirit of God, because His spirit now dwells in our mortal bodies and our minds are under the authority of our master, Jesus, we are a living, breathing, walking resemblance and manifestation of Jesus. We are hated for Christ's sake. We are hated because we are as Christ.

Satan's purpose in sending demons to attack us has one aim: to lure us out of the ark of safety. Satan knows that he cannot attack us as long as the hedge of protection, the blood of Jesus, encamps about us. He not only must seek permission, but he must have sufficient grounds for his request. When we (our soul, flesh, spirit) battle, it is because we have stepped out of the "ark of safety." God is just. If we sin, Satan has legal grounds to request access to us. Again, Satan cannot pull us out of the ark of safety; he lures us out through deception because of our pride. Satan did not pull the apple off the tree and give it to Eve. He tricked *her* into doing it, and after Adam sinned with her, he legally became their master. In spite of these battles, the Bible declares that there is rest for our souls in Jesus. We are hid in Christ, and the battle is not ours; it is the Lord's.

God uses our body to accomplish His will in the earth. The

devil seeks to destroy our body so that we cannot accomplish God's will upon the earth. God desires to place His power in us so that we can successfully complete the assignment that He has called us to in the earth, to bring others into the saving knowledge of Jesus Christ and to have life everlasting. Satan desires to place his demonic, destructive power in us so that we can successfully complete *his* assignment, which is to destroy others before ultimately being destroyed ourselves. The battle is for power. The forces are good versus evil. The prize is the possession of the souls of men. The end result is eternity. God desires and operates in truth. Satan desires and operates in deception. Truth brings life; deception brings death. Choose ye this day whom you will serve._

Chapter 22

BROKEN BREAD AND
POURED-OUT WINE

*L*ORD, TEACH ME *to pray. Give me a burden for people.* Prayer is only understood in the sense of the specific nature in which God has revealed prayer to the individual. Many gifts are given in the body of Christ for the edifying of the church. Some have been given the gift of intercession, and their primary purpose as identified by God is to intercede by making petitions before God on the behalf of others. While God may use others primarily in other areas, such as in the prophetic, they may yet still minister in the area of intercession, but not by means of making petitions on behalf of others. Rather, their ministry is through being made broken bread and poured-out wine. God, in the process of breaking and then putting us back together again, has not only allowed us to experience things others could not have endured, but after having brought us out of that ordeal he also uses it to minister into the lives of others.

You have gone through it, and the anointing that has resulted from that experience has become medicine for someone else. You are, in fact, praying or interceding for that person, but instead of doing it in the form of petitions, you are actually bearing the burden for that person.

In the Gospels we read that Jesus prayed often. Although there are several mentions of Jesus going away or going into the temple to pray, there was only one recorded prayer of intercession, and that was the public prayer to God on behalf of the disciples. While in ministry, Jesus mostly prayed privately, and yet He publicly bore the reproach of men. This is intercession in its greatest definition, for the express purpose of fulfilling God's will of restoring man back to God. Jesus was full of virtue, full of the presence and the power of God—so much so that the need of the petitioner was granted on his or her behalf without Jesus ever mumbling a word in prayer but simply at His command. Jesus lived in a constant state of intercession by His life. His deeds always mirrored His love for others. His life showed a preference for others above Himself.

WHAT IS INTERCESSION?

Intercession is the state of preferring someone else's freedom, deliverance, and healing at the expense of the exhaustion of self. To intercede for someone is to be willing to die to see the prayer request manifested in his or her life. Intercession is more than the act of making verbal petitions before God. It is surrendering yourself as a burnt offering in making the petition. It is in essence saying, "Place the burden on me instead."

An example of this is Moses telling God that if He would not deliver the people, then he wished God to blot his name out of His book. Another example is Esther saying, "If I perish, I perish":

> And it came to pass on the morrow, that Moses said unto the people, Ye have sinned a great sin: and now I will go up unto the LORD; peradventure I shall make an atonement for your sin. And Moses returned unto the LORD, and said, Oh, this people have sinned a great sin, and have made them gods of gold. Yet now, if thou wilt forgive their sin—; and if not, blot me, I pray thee,

out of thy book which thou hast written. And the LORD said unto Moses, Whosoever hath sinned against me, him will I blot out of my book.

—EXODUS 32:30–33

Go, gather together all the Jews that are present in Shushan, and fast ye for me, and neither eat nor drink three days, night or day: I also and my maidens will fast likewise; and so will I go in unto the king, which is not according to the law: and if I perish, I perish.

—ESTHER 4:16

When Jesus was placed on the cross, He actually bore our sins, our burdens. He was making eternal petitions, intercession of the greatest magnitude. He was not only making requests to God for us, but He sacrificed Himself for us. He became broken bread and poured-out wine for us.

When the disciples asked Jesus to teach them to pray, He said, "After this manner therefore pray ye: Our Father which art in heaven, Hallowed be thy name. Thy Kingdom come, Thy will be done" (Matt. 6:9–10). This was not a prayer of, "Grant my petition," but it was a prayer of, "Grant me the ability to perform *Your will*." Every area of our life must conform to the reality that our life is not our own. We have been bought with a price; we are now slaves purchased by God by His own blood. We are counted as sheep for the slaughter. Our aim, our desire, our breath in life is to do the will of the Father. Jesus said:

Jesus saith unto them, My meat is to do the will of him that sent me, and to finish his work.

—JOHN 4:34

Jesus told the disciples that whenever they ate this bread and drank this wine, representing His body and His blood, they were to do it in remembrance of Him.

WHY COMMUNION?

Communion has become a type of ceremony in the church. The apostolic doctrine holds to the pattern given in the New Testament and ritualistically carries out the acts performed by them. The emphasis is not placed on the purpose, except to remind the people that they who take of this communion unworthily "eateth and drinketh unto themselves damnation." This leaves the person to believe simply that if he or she has unconfessed sin, then he or she must not partake of this communion.

But there is a very important understanding of Communion that is almost always left out in the ceremonial practice. The minister often neglects to inform the people of this truth: When Jesus ate with the disciples (the Last Supper), He told them that He would no longer be with them in the physical state. He admonished them to understand, before proceeding any further, the cup from which they would have to drink to follow Him. He told them of the future events, how they would be persecuted for His sake, and how they must be willing, as He was, to lose their lives for their belief in Him. This sacrifice would mean a total denial of self. The partaking of Jesus's blood and His body would symbolize a blood covenant between the disciples and Jesus. They would no longer be able to live independently of Jesus. Not only that, but if they brought a reproach to Him (or betrayed Him), they would be in danger of bringing destruction upon themselves.

For he that eateth and drinketh unworthily, eateth and drinketh damnation to himself, not discerning the Lord's body.

—1 CORINTHIANS 11:29

Communion serves as an open acknowledgement of identification with and full surrender to the person of Jesus Christ. To make a public declaration of surrender to Jesus and then privately humiliate and denounce Him by actions is very dangerous.

For this cause many are weak and sickly among you, and may sleep.

—1 CORINTHIANS 11:30

HIDDEN TREASURES

Jesus did not come to this world to give us heaven on Earth. He came to disciple prophets, preachers, teachers, and evangelists for the perfecting of the saints and for the work of the ministry. Yes, there are fringe benefits to surrender and obedience to Christ, but it is not the cause. It is simply the effect. Jesus said, "I came that you might have life, and have it more abundantly." (See John 10:10.) Jesus came to give us eternal life, a life that surpasses our human understanding, one filled with glories and riches untold. But, in our human life He also came to give us depth. That is why in Mark 8:35 we read that Jesus asked what it profits a man to gain the whole world and lose his soul.

A man does not just simply die and then go to hell. He is born dead. Instead of the body having been raised with Christ, it stays dead, rotting and decaying. In the ancient times, royal men and women were buried with their treasures. They were treated with expensive oils and spices and were adorned in beautiful garments and covered with precious jewels and gems. There treasures were oftentimes placed in the tombs with them. This ritual is quite comparable to the rich man who is still physically alive, but because he is without God, is spiritually dead. He has the mansion, he has the fine cars, he has the servants and wives, and his every wish is at his command. Yet, he is "dead" and unable to enjoy his riches. Not only does he not enjoy them while physically alive, but he dies, and someone else who has less worldly wisdom but has become foolish for God enjoys the fruit of his labor.

King Solomon says it this way:

> For there is a man whose labour is in wisdom, and in knowledge, and in equity; yet to a man that hath not laboured therein shall he leave it for his portion. This also is vanity and a great evil.
>
> —ECCLESIASTES 2:21

We have been chosen and are being prepared for the Master's use. Unless we have committed ourselves to be broken bread and poured-out wine for Jesus, our life is but a vapor, having no substance. We are as walking dead.

Chapter 23

I'VE GONE TOO FAR TO
TURN BACK NOW

And it came to pass, when they had brought them forth abroad, that
he said, Escape for thy life; look not behind thee, neither stay thou in
all the plain; escape to the mountain, lest thou be consumed.... But
his wife looked back from behind him, and she became a pillar of salt.

—GENESIS 19:17, 26

And Jesus said unto him, No man, having put his hand to the
plough, and looking back, is fit for the kingdom of God.

—LUKE 9:62

G OD IS NO longer asking, but He is demanding that a line be drawn in the sand. The wheat and the tare have been allowed to grow together, but now it's harvest time, and the harvester has come out to pick his crops. God has told us to "come out from among them, and be ye separate" (2 Cor. 6:17).

> For men shall be lovers of their own selves, covetous, boasters, proud, blasphemers, disobedient to parents, unthankful, unholy, Without natural affection, truce-breakers, false accusers, incontinent, fierce, despisers of those that are good, Traitors, heady, highminded, lovers of pleasures more than lovers of God; Having a form of godliness, but denying the power thereof: from such turn away. For of this sort are they which

creep into houses, and lead captive silly women laden
with sins, led away with divers lusts, Ever learning, and
never able to come to the knowledge of the truth. Now
as Jannes and Jambres withstood Moses, so do these
also resist the truth: men of corrupt minds, reprobate
concerning the faith.

—2 TIMOTHY 3:2–8

One of the biggest deceptions of the enemy is to continuously cause us to see these people as people of the world;
therefore, we avoid interactions with the world at all cost,
even to the point of ministering to the unsaved. We have concluded that if God doesn't bring them into our space, then it
is not His desire for them to be saved. The devil is a liar!

The Bible is speaking directly to the church. In Revelation,
Jesus gave instructions to several churches. He was not at all
speaking to the world; His chastisement was to the church.

Jesus answered them, Have not I chosen you twelve,
and one of you is a devil? He spake of Judas Iscariot
the son of Simon: for he it was that should betray him,
being one of the twelve.

—JOHN 6:70–71

The flesh is enmity against God. No man can come unto
God unless He draws him. We are without *any* desire for
God in and of ourselves. Although our being testifies of His
existence and the "knowing" is within us, we do not desire
Him. We know that God is real, but our lustful nature rejects
godly interference. We want His salvation, but we want it
on our terns. If we can't have this God on our terms, then
forget it! The Bible declares that no man can come to God
except He draws him (John 6:44). It is important to realize
that many who are drawn or given the opportunity to come

I've Gone Too Far to Turn Back Now

to Christ still refuse to be transformed by His presence, even once they have encountered it. Satan did not get to earth and then rebel against God; he rebelled while he was still in heaven. He rebelled while in God's presence. It is one thing, like Saul of Tarsus, to be a sinner in ignorance, but to come into the knowledge of and presence of Jesus Christ with no condemnation of sin, to stand in complete arrogance in the face of the Holy One, is complete and total rebellion.

131

Chapter 24

THE DEFEATED GERM

When Jesus heard that, he said, This sickness is not unto death, but
for the glory of God, that the Son of God might be glorified thereby.
—JOHN 11:4

Jesus answered, Neither hath this man sinned, nor his parents:
but that the works of God should be made manifest in him.
—JOHN 9:3

D O WE NOT yet understand who Jesus is, who we are
inside of Him? Remember the little boy who cowered
in the presence of his bullies, only to return with his
big brother and talk smack to the bullies from behind his
brother's back? Precisely. We are because Christ is. Our life's
crisis is for all intents and purposes so that Christ might be
raised up in us and glorified through us in the presence of
those around us.

Jesus almost always had witnesses. There were some occa-
sions where He healed someone and told that person not to
tell anyone, but in his or her excitement, he or she did so
anyway. These witnesses were people who had known of the
victim whom God used. They could verify the validity of
their ailment and the length of time the thorn existed. The
victims, however, were people who had been talked about,
teased, taunted, and cast out of the popular circles. These
were people whose own families had disowned them, who

saw them as strange and peculiar people. In our own experiences as victims, we did not understand that God was allowing the disfigurement in our lives so that He could be glorified in our future deliverance.

THE INFECTION

In the research to find a cure for cancer, animals are injected with the disease so that they become infected. This infestation is necessary to find a cure. Without a cause, there is no effect. What would Jesus deliver us from if we had not had problems? Why would we feel that we needed Him if we were all right? Psychologists spend a great deal of the therapy with patients getting them to identify the source of the problem. However, before therapy can begin, the patient must admit that he or she has a problem. Once the problem has been identified, then the cure is imminent, and the patient has found the necessary barrier to prevent a relapse.

How would the people in our lives and those we come in contact with know the powerful working power of Jesus in our lives, except that we had a history of problems (lasting over a long period of time) that are not only verified but could only be healed by Jesus? Yet, the moment the revelation of the person of Jesus became real to us, our mortal bodies were quickened by the power of Jesus's resurrection, and we were set free.

The truth of the scriptures is that every evil, every sin, every illness is subject to and must bow to the person and presence of Jesus Christ. It is not simply that Jesus was empowered by God to do these miracles, but rather He was the embodiment of God, empowered by Himself. His presence commanded sin and its manifestations to bow.

And these signs shall follow them that believe; In my name shall they cast out devils; they shall speak with new tongues; They shall take up serpents; and if they drink any deadly thing, it shall not hurt them; they shall lay hands on the sick, and they shall recover.

—MARK 16:17–18

Like the blood in our veins brings life into our mortal bodies, so the Spirit flowing in our body brings life to our spiritual body. This phenomenon produces the spiritual individual seen and recognized only by spiritual beings.

THE BARRIER

This Holy Spirit flowing through us serves as a barrier to protect us against any foreign agent. No sickness or disease can penetrate that barrier. If that barrier has been penetrated through sin then it is obvious that the flow ceases. There has been a blockage, and death is imminent. When the blood flow is hampered in the human body, as in the hardening of the arteries, physical death is imminent unless the blood flow can be resumed. So it is in the spirit. The spiritual flow must be resumed to restore the spiritual life and its protective barrier.

The Bible says that we are hidden in Christ. When the devil comes after us, he finds a protective shield that cannot be penetrated, which is the blood of Jesus. It is our life force. No foreign agency can cross over the blood of Jesus. We are visible to the eye, yet untouchable. We are, in human definition, hidden. We must be lured out of the hidden place or away from this protective shield through sin or unbelief if we are to be consumed.

Over and over again, the Scriptures show us lives transformed after coming into the presence of Jesus—lives transformed by Christ even though illnesses had been verified, deaths were several days old, and illnesses were present at birth. Without question, the presence of God alone brings forth healing, but there is yet another matter: The question is not whether or not Jesus can heal, but rather, does He desire to? I know that Jesus is Lord. I know that He can heal the sick, return sight to the blind, heal the brokenhearted, and release the captives. I have seen Him do these things for other people, but I struggle to accept that He will do it for me. I say, "There is a penalty to sin, and I must pay full price."

As he did with Jesus, Satan will tell us these half-truths. He will indeed quote the Scriptures to convince us of his lies, and he will distort the Scriptures or leave out portions of it. The Scriptures say, "For the wages of sin is death; but the gift of God is eternal life through Jesus Christ our Lord" (Rom. 6:23). Sin entered into the world through the disobedience of Adam and Eve, and physical death is imminent. Yet, eternal life is available through Jesus. Before you grew up and committed those sinful acts, you were already condemned. Your sinful acts did not add to your condemnation, so there is nothing that you have done to put yourself in this sinful state. You were 100 percent guilty the moment you came out of your mother's womb. Not believing that Jesus will forgive those hideous deeds that you committed at an age of accountability is the same as not believing that Jesus will forgive and save an infant who dies in infancy. The difference is, you are now old enough to make the request and to decipher the alternatives, and the infant (through the grace of God) gets the decision made for him.

Forgiveness Through Christ

For many of us, it is easier to believe God to forgive you for your sins and to cleanse you from the physical manifestations of the sin than it is to believe that this Man, whose seed was from God, miraculously entered into the womb of a virgin girl and was born of flesh, that He lived thirty years without ever committing sin and is now seated with God in heaven as our Mediator. However, in order to receive a portion of the truth, you must receive all of it. This same Jesus died so that you might have life, and that more abundantly. He took the stripes upon Himself that were due you so that you could be healed. Jesus defeated that germ that desires to invade your person. If you believe it, this protective shield is yours.

> Jesus said unto him, If thou canst believe, all things are possible to him that believeth.
>
> —Mark 9:23

In this passage, we see Jesus telling the disciples that all things were possible if they believed. It is not enough to have the protective shield of the Holy Ghost if you don't believe it is so. Not being totally convinced of this truth will cause you to be deceived into relinquishing it.

On the other hand, those who come in contact with this holy presence without the desire or intent to be transformed will run in terror from its presence. They will label this presence as "the spirit of Beelzebub." (See Matthew 12:24–28.) Since this experience is not understandable by human intellect or insight, it is attributed to demons. Now, we're in jeopardy of blasphemy. When we make this error in attribution, we have contributed the work of the Holy Spirit to the work of the devil.

Chapter 25

THE FELLOWSHIP OF CHRIST'S SUFFERING

That I may know him, and the power of his resurrection, and the fellowship of his sufferings, being made conformable unto his death.

—PHILIPPIANS 3:10

W HEN WE TALK about submitting our life to Jesus, we're talking about being in the fellowship of Christ's life. The ceremony of baptism represents an intention to become identified with the death of Jesus Christ in all areas of our life and to identify with the Resurrection in the newness of life, or in the image of Jesus.

LIVING WATER

Every physical response has a twin spiritual response. The spiritual things are made manifest in the flesh. The totality of the spiritual endowment at baptism will so consume the flesh that the glory of God fills the temple (the flesh) and the vocal chords, and the speech will be as a fountain of living water. The Word declares that out of our belly shall flow rivers of living water (John 7:38). This is the fullness of Christ in our flesh expanding from out of our flesh. When this happens, it is no more I, but it is Christ who liveth in me (Gal. 2:20). I have now been conformed to the image of Christ. I have been transformed, because I have renewed my mind.

How have I renewed my mind? I have purposely and intentionally changed my desire by changing my master. I have purposely defied the law of nature. In other words, I have denied the innate dictates of the flesh (through crucifying the flesh) and have instead forced and commanded the flesh to obey the Spirit of God in me in order to be transformed and become obedient to the person of Jesus. I refuse the desires of the flesh, the world's riches, intelligence, goals, and standards, The Word instructs us to bring our own bodies under subjection, yet in contrast it is actually Christ who works in us to perform His good pleasure.

WHO'S IN CHARGE?

Do I do it, or does Christ do it? Well, I don't know exactly what it is that Christ wants to do in and through my body, so I can't help him do what I don't know. What I can do is prepare my body for whatever Jesus's purpose is by commanding it to obey only the Spirit of God in it. This is my soulish realm. This is my mind. We're not talking about my arms, my legs, and my mouth. We're talking about my mind. As I, through the power of my will, yield this powerful entity, my mind (soul), to Jesus, He in turn works out the purpose for which He designed my soul or my mind, and consequently my body follows.

This transformation must truly confuse the physical body. This body is in disarray, wondering what in the world is happening. Ah, the answer was, as only Paul can explain, "There is a war in my members. I know how to defeat this flesh once and for all. I will walk in the spirit, and therefore I will not fulfill the lust of the flesh. I will purposely and aggressively bring my body and mind under subjection to the obedience

The Fellowship of Christ's Suffering

of Jesus. I will incline my ear unto the Lord, and I will see through the eyes of Christ.

"But this earth and the fullness of the sin in it dictates to my flesh the necessities of life by its standards. I am not only become a stranger in the land of which I was born, but the multitudes abiding in this land with me have become my enemies. They see me as a strange creature, not belonging. By the dictates of their limited knowledge, coupled with the world's acceptable standards for living, I am out of place. I don't fit in and have thereby become a nuisance to them.

"As Jesus is resurrected in the fullness of me, more of the person of Jesus and the power of his resurrection show forth from me as a fountain that brings conviction and condemnation to everyone who passes this stream. However, through deception, these blinded eyes do not, therefore, see the person or presence of Christ, but an enemy, sent to destroy them. And, at the same time, there is yet an aura of truth and righteousness overflowing from this vessel that those passing by cannot deny." (See Romans chapters 7–8.)

UNDERSTANDING GOD

It is not my command or job to decipher this phenomenon or to explain it. That is Christ's job. We spend a great deal of time attempting to explain the things of God, which are unexplainable. Thus the reason much of the New Testament is written in parables. The Bible focuses on real-life situations in order to bring us into an understanding of our spiritual Creator. God used a physical Christ with love overflowing, crucified and tormented without cause with the retaliation of love to show us Himself. God has to show us Himself (the reality) through our humanness (the vapor). This earthly realm, for us, seems true, and God is a vapor. The opposite is,

141

in fact, true. This earthly realm is a vapor, and God is true. God's love caused Him to wrap Himself in flesh and enter this realm of vapor to show us His truth by using our level of understanding and comprehension to do it. Now we're without excuse: "Choose you this day whom ye will serve" (Josh. 24:15).

THE PROPHET OF THE LORD

How would I understand what I have done against my Lord unless if by parable there was a life experience to make the comparison? I could use someone else's life situation to bring the point of the parable to life, but how would I know the hurt or the love without the personal experience? The Book of Hosea was written for the purpose of using a real-life experience to show the people of Israel how they had become harlots by giving themselves to other gods. Why did this prophet's life have to be filled with so much pain to bring this point to life?

We must understand God's definition of a prophet in contrast with the world's definition. The world seeks out the prophet of the Lord as they seek out fortune-tellers. They want someone to tell them of the future blessings that God has for them. They want someone to "pat them on the back" for a job well done, and they want to be openly praised before the people so that people would look at them in awe and glorify them. God's definition of a prophet is "one who delivers a divine message from God." God not only uses the mouthpiece of the chosen prophet, but more often than not He allows the prophet to portray the words that God wants spoken, as an actress plays out a part in a movie scene.

There are, however, a few situations in which God allowed the prophet to experience the message he or she delivered afterward, as was the case with Jonah. When Jonah *finally* obeyed God and spoke the message to the people, the people repented, and God did not bring judgment upon that generation. Jonah was angry because he felt that if God were going to spare them anyway, why take him through the unnecessary inconvenience of relaying the message? God in His infinite wisdom allowed Jonah to experience His grace when He covered Jonah from the hot sun with a large leaf, but later God allowed the worm to eat the leaf, exposing Jonah to the sun again. God's point to Jonah was that Jonah welcomed God's grace because God's wrath was unbearable, and so it was with the people to whom God had Jonah deliver the message. The people appreciated God's grace and, as a result, returned to God.

Whether before the inspired Word of God is given in direction or after the fact, God, it seems, almost always—if not always—causes His prophets to experience the word they will deliver. The prophet speaks with authority and great conviction, and the prophet not only speaks the word of the Lord but has a great burden for the people and purpose of God. They have to first become acquainted with the seriousness of the message God wants delivered.

WHEN GOD CHOOSES YOU

Jesus, our great Intercessor, first became acquainted with the grief and sufferings of the people before He would bring about our salvation. Why is it that Jesus was thirty years old before going forth into ministry? What was he doing those thirty years? What was Moses doing those forty years before his ministry began? What were Abraham, Elisha, Joseph, Jonah, Ezekiel, Isaiah, John the Baptist, Paul, and so many others doing before they were thrust forward into ministry?

They were becoming acquainted with the grief and sufferings of the people. When these chosen vessels moved into the prophetic ministry, they went forth with a strong burden for the people. They had lived the message before they proclaimed it. So it is with God's people today. A true prophet of the Lord will live a message before he proclaims it, and it will be undeniably the Word of the Lord!

Those who live holy lives shall suffer persecution, but God cautioned us not to suffer because of a wrong that we have done but for Jesus's sake. If we are suffering for the wrong we've committed, then so be it. But if we are suffering for the cause of Christ, then rejoice in the suffering and the impending reward and the holy retribution of the suffering.

Chapter 26

THE MOTIVE IS LOVE

S O, THEN, WHY would anyone choose to suffer? For love! God's motive is always love.

That he would grant you, according to the riches of his glory, to be strengthened with might by his Spirit in the inner man; That Christ may dwell in your hearts by faith; that ye, being rooted and grounded in love, May be able to comprehend with all saints what is the breadth, and length, and depth, and height; And to know the love of Christ, which passeth knowledge, that ye might be filled with all the fulness of God.

—EPHESIANS 3:16–19

It is not until we realize the love of Christ for us that we can live victoriously. Our love for Him is not really love, because it is flesh. It is imperfect and has flaws. More importantly, it is conditional. When we really come to an understanding of the unconditional love that the Father has for us through His Son Jesus, then and only then can we begin to love Him back.

As a result of our sin nature, Christ knew that we would only love Him if He showed how much He loved us first. The Scriptures say, "Herein is love, not that we loved God, but that he loved us" (1 John 4:10). This love is only made great when we realize *who* it is that loves us. In my devotional time with my Lord, I was enjoying His presence so much that I told

Him that I wanted to come home and be with Him, and His answer to me was, "Bev, glorify me in your body." The one thing that I have heard ringing the loudest is in my spirit is the command to love! I know that God has placed His love in me so that He can use this vessel and be revealed through it to perform exactly what He desires. God is taking this vessel and preparing it for His use. But He is doing more than that. He is pouring out His Spirit upon me, and He is transforming me into His image. Like Moses, His glory will shine forth from me as a great light. That glory is absolute love. God's very nature is love, and the light that shines from you is the physical manifestation of His love. Love has no description. When people speak of seeing Jesus, they are speaking of His love. Their description of Him is love, and His purpose in us is to show love to those around us so intensely that they are totally unable to see us, but see only Him.

Just like you can see a demon in someone, yet his or her physical features still remain, so it is with the God's love. You can see Jesus in people, yet their physical features haven't changed. That is why the disciples and Mary did not immediately recognize Jesus after His resurrection. Jesus had taken on a supernatural form. Yet, when Jesus revealed Himself as flesh, He was recognizable. Jesus is recognized by those to whom He "chooses" to reveal Himself, but He uses a physical body to do this. You see, man looks at the outer appearance, but God looks at the heart (or spirit, the real person). God is a spirit, and they who worship Him must worship Him in spirit and in truth. It is through our spirit man that others see Jesus in us, not our physical body.

What is God's purpose for my life? To have me so identified with Christ that when someone looks at me, they see Jesus. That Christ is recognizable in me, that the character, the personality, the demeanor of Jesus is made manifest in my mortal body.

I AND THE FATHER ARE ONE

When Jesus spoke with the disciples, He said that when they had seen Him, they had seen the Father. Jesus was so identified with God that at any point and time, God was revealed in Him. Jesus portrayed the character, personality, thoughts, intents, desires, dislikes, and concerns of God. That's why He said that when we had seen Him we had seen the Father. He did what the Father told Him to do.

We are to do what Jesus wants, or what He tells us to do. The Bible says that God so loved the world that He gave us His only begotten Son (John 3:16). Jesus was a living manifestation of God's love for us. Our person is to be a living manifestation of God's love for us *and* for others. In other words, Jesus's birth was for the purpose of expressing God's heart toward us, and our rebirth is for the purpose of expressing Jesus's death, burial, and resurrection so that we may express God's love toward others. I was born for the purpose of expressing the love of Christ to men, yet I cannot express this love unless it is yielded to the One who does the expressing. We are to be so identified with Jesus that at any point in time Jesus can be revealed in us.

Chapter 27

NO MORE I, BUT CHRIST

I am crucified with Christ: nevertheless I live; yet not I, but Christ liveth in me: and the life which I now live in the flesh I live by the faith of the Son of God, who loved me, and gave himself for me.

—GALATIANS 2:20

E KNOW IN theory that we are alive in Christ and dead indeed to sin, but in actuality we live in this world. We exist in this human realm with human expectations and demands, trials, tests, and temptations. We awake in the morning, and the reality of this world's issues are awaiting us. In our mind, it is not the Christ in me who has to deal with the employer, the disgruntled mate, and the rebellious children. I, through my human senses, must handle these issues on a daily basis. How do I live in Christ yet in this world simultaneously?

> For ye are bought with a price: therefore glorify God in your body, and in your spirit, which are God's.
>
> —1 CORINTHIANS 6:20

The issue here is really an issue of the heart (the human will). The concept of glorifying God in our body is so difficult because we do not really want to glorify God in our bodies. We don't really want to yield our members to Christ. The difficulty is not in the ability; it is in the desire. Those who live in the flesh desire to obey the dictates of the flesh. We want salvation, we want forgiveness, we want to live eternally in heaven, but we also want all and everything that this world has to offer.

I have heard many people teach that "once saved, always saved." The concept in this statement is that the unregenerate individual pays for his other sins and trespasses in this world so that he or she can go to heaven cleansed. Now I'm confused.

The Bible declares:

> Know ye not that the unrighteous shall not inherit the kingdom of God? Be not deceived: neither fornicators, nor idolaters, nor adulterers, nor effeminate, nor abusers of themselves with mankind, Nor thieves, nor covetous, nor drunkards, nor revilers, nor extortioners, shall inherit the kingdom of God.
>
> —1 CORINTHIANS 6:9–10

So then whom do 1 believe? People or the Word of God? The answer, as only the Holy Spirit can reveal, is simply that those traits and characteristics that prevent our going to heaven were placed on our Lord in our place on the cross and destroyed. When we are born again, we are new creatures in Christ Jesus. We are no longer the people of 1 Corinthians. We have once and for all been saved, but the real question is, Do we believe that Jesus paid it all, and have we in response to that belief been crucified with Christ and raised with Him in the newness of life?

THE ENEMY'S DECEPTION

The scripture passage starts out by saying, "Be not deceived [mislead]" (1 Cor. 6:9). The statement suggests that to believe opposite of what that scripture states is to be deceived. Well, man has an argument for every interpretation. Man can always take a scripture out of context to validate his deception. So let's for a moment just use common sense. If God is a holy God, He is upright. If that is true, then it stands to reason that the stench of sin would sicken Him. We know that God cannot be in the presence of sin, and even had to turn from His own Son when the sins of the world were placed upon Him. So the common sense argument would be, Jesus carried all of our sins, past, present, and future to the cross, which destroyed the power of the sin. The gift of God is life eternal, and since it is a gift, no work is needed to obtain it.

The evil, selfish, self-centered person desires what pleases only himself and values others based on their service to him. You pay for what you want. Some of us pay with money, some pay with sexual favors, others the pretension of love and emotional support. So, then, your relationships are based on a reciprocal process. Our expectations are really out of a heart or root of pride and arrogance, a sense that you are deserving of reciprocation. A prideful individual has a false sense of humility, when the truth is the acts of kindness have attached to it a reciprocal demand.

In the humble man, if someone jeopardizes his or her life to save his, or sacrifices something of great value for you, you are indebted to that person. You want to show your appreciation for what was done on your behalf, knowing full well that you did not deserve such love. The humility in the man or woman loved, redeemed, saved by God, causes him or her to say, "I know that I do not deserve such wonderful treatment, such unconditional love, because I was evil, wicked, prideful, and arrogant. Therefore, in appreciation, I will spend the rest of my life saying thank you. My life will be a daily walk of gratitude, and I will shout from the rooftops the goodness of this One who saved my life. My reasonable service in appreciation is to present my body a living sacrifice, holy and acceptable." This is the bare minimum!

MY BODY, A LIVING SACRIFICE

One who does not present his or her body a living sacrifice to seek to please the One who loved him or her unconditionally is the one who does not have gratitude and appreciation for the love shown to them. That person has not accepted this love; he or she has rejected it. So then, they have rejected the Lover, the Giver; they have rejected God. How can one enter into the kingdom of God if he or she has rejected the King? I am indebted to the One who saved me, who rescued me from the enemies of the spirit world, the enemies of the natural world, and the enemies of self. I was doomed and am now rescued. I was saved!

Now, in order to remain in the ark of safety there is something I must do. Evil still desires to overtake and destroy me; therefore I must hide and remain hidden. Where will I hide?

> For ye are dead, and your life is hid with Christ in God.
>
> —COLOSSIANS 3:3

So then, if I am hidden in Christ, then it is no more *me*. It is *Christ*. The life I now live, I live in Christ. If one is hidden, he cannot be seen. This is a very real statement. If people can still see us (our old nature, our old character, and not the character of Christ), then it is clear that Christ has not overtaken our mortal bodies. When Jesus spoke, He was a man, clothed in flesh.

There was nothing extraordinary about Jesus's personal appearance, yet when He appeared before John the Baptist, He was recognized as the Savior of the world.

The next day John seeth Jesus coming unto him, and saith, Behold the Lamb of God, which taketh away the sin of the world.

—JOHN 1:29

Jesus glorified God in His flesh. God in Christ was seen through the flesh of Jesus.

ENTERTAINING ANGELS

The Bible tells us to be careful, that we may be entertaining angels unaware. How many of us have been in the presence of angels and knew it? I can remember one occurrence when an angel walked into our church and began to speak with us. Everyone circled around this man in awe of him. They didn't know why they were so drawn to this stranger, but they were astounded at his words and his presence. I stood in the background, knowing immediately that this was an angel. I ran to go and get the pastor to inform him that an angel was in our midst, but when I returned the angel had left. I said to the pastor, "Pastor, that was an angel." He smiled at me gently, and everyone went on about his or her business. I was amazed that no one knew this but me.

Likewise, there is something about the presence of the Lord that is unmistakable, but as awesome as the presence of the Lord is, one can be in the midst of Him and not recognize Him.

And it came to pass, that, while they communed together and reasoned, Jesus himself drew near, and went with them. But their eyes were holden that they should not know him.

—LUKE 24:15–16

I am convinced that the presence of the Lord brings imme-
diate deliverance, healing, and revelation. Many times God
does not instantly bring either of the above to people. He
allows only our flesh as intercessors to confer with their flesh.
However, when God desires to commune with individuals,
to bring deliverance, healing, or revelation into their lives,
he will quicken our mortal bodies. Like the disciples, rather
than see "the man," their eyes will open to see the Jesus in us.

OUR TEMPLE

This flesh, our bodies, the temple of the Lord must be prepared. The table must be set. The atmosphere must be condu-
cive for the Lord's presence. We place so much emphasis on the
building as the temple or place of worship unto the Lord, but
God places the emphasis on our body as the temple of the Lord.
We build great edifices and tabernacles, and like the temple in
Jerusalem, we prostitute the temple of the Lord for the praise
and acceptance of man. We allow men to come into the house
of the Lord with their ideas of profit and gain. These people
justify these evil acts by saying they are doing these things to
advance the kingdom of God, as in this story in Matthew:

> And Jesus went into the temple of God, and cast out
> all them that sold and bought in the temple, and over-
> threw the tables of the moneychangers, and the seats of
> them that sold doves, And said unto them, It is written,
> My house shall be called the house of prayer; but ye
> have made it a den of thieves.
>
> —MATTHEW 21:12–13

In my youth I can remember the church being known for
its barbeque dinners, its pies and cakes, its yard sales and
the like, in the name of the Lord. Do we not yet know that

God All-Powerful knows how to get money for Himself if He desires? It is God who gives power to get wealth (Deut. 8:18). God need only speak to the heart of the wealthy to bless whom He chooses or to build his temple.

David, a man I have spoken of a great deal in this book, desired to build God a temple (1 Chron. 17). God responded to David through the Prophet Nathan that God would indeed build David a house, and his house would be established forever. God indeed established His own house, His temple, but God spoke of a temple not built with hands. This temple is in the bodies of those who yield themselves unto Him. The tangible blessings these individuals receive are simply outward manifestations of the person yielded to Christ. The tangible blessings are not the glory of God, as the glory of God is found in the person, not the manifestation.

Too often we glory in the manifestation of Jesus, but not in Jesus. We foolishly refuse to accept that there is no glory outside of Christ. Men and women of God chosen and used by God mightily have been guilty of attributing the gifts of operation through them to their efforts. They want the people to recognize, admonish, and glory in them. They do not want the people to see Christ but them. So then, the spirit of the Lord leaves that person, as with King Saul, who was anointed by God, became puffed up, and had his anointing removed by God. Not only did that happen, but God gave permission to an unclean spirit to torment King Saul as a result of his disobedient heart.

Jesus hung on the cross for six hours. Once He died, His seed of righteousness fell to the ground and died. The seed took root and sprang forth. Many of us have been hanging on the tree for many years. It's time to die and become a seed that Christ might spring forth through our mortal bodies. All glory, all honor, and all praise *must* go to our Lord and Savior, Jesus Christ. No more I, but Christ who lives in me.

Chapter 28

WHO WAS I BEFORE THE LIE?

G OD CREATED MAN in His image and in His likeness. Sin defiled the likeness of God in man, but Jesus's death and resurrection gave it back to us. As a result of this sinful nature and the length of time and generations in which we carried this sin nature, getting the lie out of us is a lengthy process, and putting the truth back into us takes even longer. It is important to understand that truth cannot be imputed to us until the lie has been purged out of us. It is not until we see the lie through the continuous destruction of it that we even accept it as such.

The sin nature fortifies our sinful bodies, and vice versa, and the sinful earth produces nourishment (bread) needed for our sinful desires. In other words, fruit in and of itself that was created for the sinless body does not satisfy man. Our nature craves desires and requests destructive things. Man desires processed food, developed by the sinful man, which is destructive to the body, rather than the fruit produced by a sinless God for a sinless man, producing life to the body.

Although the redemptive work of Christ on the cross was for the purpose of bringing us back into right relationship with our Father God, we were without a desire for Him. The Bibles declares that no man can come unto Christ except He draws him. Simply put, in and of ourselves, we do not have a desire to know Christ. It is in the simplicity of accepting the redemptive work of Christ on the cross without knowing the details that the process of purging begins in our life. It is the compulsion to answer the call—and only that—that causes us to come into a relationship with Christ.

THE AGONY OF THE CROSS

At the foot of the cross we see God's wisdom. We see God reconciling the world unto Himself. We see God there glorious in holiness; fearful in praise; doing wonders; and simultaneously forgiving iniquity, transgression, and sin. Isaiah 53 speaks of God's wisdom when the prophet states:

> Yet it pleased the LORD to bruise him; he hath put him to grief: when thou shalt make his soul an offering for sin, he shall see his seed, he shall prolong his days, and the pleasure of the LORD shall prosper in his hand.
>
> —ISAIAH 53:10

We see God's grace, and we ask, Why did you give your only begotten Son to bleed on our behalf? For this answer we need to tell it, tell it in heaven, and publish it in all the golden streets every hour of every glorious day that such is the grace of God that He gave His only begotten Son so that whosoever believed in Him should not perish but have everlasting life.

Last, while looking up at the foot of the cross we see God's sovereignty. What sovereignty is this that the angels who fell should have no redeemer, but that man, insignificant, being fallen, should find a Savior in heaven's Only Begotten!

THE GRACE OF GOD

There is no evil repercussion; therefore, I have nothing to fear. Only the grace and the love of God will be returned to me as I, through Christ, extend the grace and love of Jesus to others. As I extend peace, only peace will come back. As I extend forgiveness, only forgiveness will come back. I shall reap what I sow, and only that which I sow. I can come out of hiding and be soft and loving. I do not have to be protective or careful. I can be free to love.

OUR FUTILITY

How often I have played dumb in the midst of the great wisdom that God has given me? I have taken the credit for this wisdom in humbly concluding that I was not worthy (in pride), exalting my abilities above God. I have tried so hard to fit in, denying myself, denying the wisdom of God in me, and ultimately denying my God. I have hidden Christ and His wisdom, only allowing Him to emerge in "comfortable" surroundings. I have told my Lord that I want Him revealed in my life only at the times that I designate. I have asked Him for power, yet I have denied the Power-Giver. I attempted to use God for my glory instead of allowing God's glory to use me. How grossly and negligently I have mishandled the blood-bought power and authority of my Lord and Savior, Jesus Christ, How patient and long-suffering my Jesus has been with me.

Oh, the prisons of life. Everything became a prison. My childhood was a prison. I looked forward to turning eighteen so that I could be released from this childhood prison, but there was yet another prison, this one for adults only! Over the years, I ended up in many different prisons, attempted many escapes, but I was caught and returned back to each one. My last attempt to escape landed me in the worst prison of all, maximum security. This prison was the prison of *self*.

After the exhaustion and frustration of many failed escape attempts, I voluntarily turned myself in and surrendered to the warden (Satan). After many years of incarceration, it occurred to me that this imprisonment was, in fact, voluntary, that I had placed myself in prison, feeling somehow that I deserved to be locked up and at the same time blaming and resenting everyone else. It was I all the time! All this time it was I who had the key to unlock my prison door. It was I who kept putting me in the cell, because that was where I felt comfortable. I was afraid to come out and face the world, so I made excuses to stay in prison, where it was safe. This prison relieved me from the duty, the responsibility, of pressing on. There was good reason why I couldn't go forth.

THE FREEING POWER OF THE BLOOD OF JESUS

Thank God for the blood of Jesus Christ. Jesus removed all excuses, all stains, and all guilt. Not only was bail posted for me by Jesus's own blood, but when I came out of the cell, someone was there waiting for me. Everything I needed to live—my income, my health, my happiness, my peace, my prosperity—was handed to me at that moment, so I was not coming into the world empty-handed. Best of all, I didn't even have to do anything to receive this gift. All I had to do was *believe* that this royal family, through no goodness of my own, had decided to adopt me. They have legally adopted me, and therefore all that is theirs is mine. I am even made an heir to this great kingdom. All I had to do was believe that it was true, take a step of faith, and walk out of that prison cell and go with them. Because Jesus, the Father, and the Holy Spirit made a joint decision to adopt me as their own, I will spend the rest of my life showing my gratitude through total obedience and submission to the will of God in my life.

> For I know the thoughts that I think toward you, saith the LORD, thoughts of peace, and not of evil, to give

you an expected end. Then shall ye call upon me, and ye shall go and pray unto me, and I will hearken unto you. And ye shall seek me, and find me, when ye shall search for me with all your heart. And I will be found of you, saith the LORD: and I will turn away your captivity, and I will gather you from all the nations, and from all the places whither I have driven you, saith the LORD; and I will bring you again into the place whence I caused you to be carried away captive.

—JEREMIAH 29:11–14

Chapter 29

NOW GLORIFY GOD IN YOUR BODY

G OD HAS BEINGS who are totally spirits (angels). He did not create us to be like the angels but to be a little lower than the angels. God created us so that His glory could be manifested in the flesh as well as the spirit in the earth. The job of the enemy is to prevent us or our bodies from possessing the ability to bring glory to God. Failed marriages, disobedient children, and sick bodies do not bring glory to God.

Christians are on some sort of spiritual plain. Many of us are trying to see how spiritual we can get so that man will glorify us for our abilities. Very few of us acquire the wisdom, knowledge, and power of God for the purpose of glorifying Him. God, in His mercy, allows us time to repent in the midst of the misuse of the gifts He has placed in us, but soon He will cut us down if we do not repent. God will literally allow you to have what you think you want, what you've worked so hard in the flesh to have, for the destruction of your body. Be careful what you ask for or seek.

Satan's very nature is deception. He has been stripped of his power by the King of kings and Lord of lords. When Jesus arose from the grave, all power in heaven and earth was given to Him. Satan operates on the limited power God gives him for the purpose of accomplishing God's will. Satan is no more master than we are. He is subject to the direction and guidance of God. Satan, in his battle against God, causes man, created in the very image of God, to bring humiliation to his Creator. Since God wants us to glorify Him in our body, Satan uses this same body to bring embarrassment to God. Satan can only bring embarrassment to God through God's chosen. Those who have not been chosen by God are really of no use to the devil except to torment the godly.

So then, Satan deceives us into believing that we are accomplishing or performing the will of God for our lives. Everyone around us may look and marvel at the great work that God is doing in and through us. They may have begun to praise and worship God for His greatness, this mirage they believe God has performed, and then when they're totally comfortable in the perceived will of God, Satan pulls off the mask. It's not really God doing this great work; it is Satan disguised.

Satan does not simply want to destroy the people of God. He wants to bring a reproach to God through the saints. He wants to show God that the character of Satan is more desired than the character of Christ. He wants to show that if the price is right, we will turn on God for him, that we will desire earthly riches over kingdom riches, that his way is more desirable to humans than their Creator's way.

SATAN'S TEMPTATIONS

Then was Jesus led up by the Spirit into the wilderness to be tested by the devil.

—MATTHEW 4:1

Satan knew from the beginning the weakness that was in the flesh. Since Satan was a spirit being he could not in himself know the challenges faced by humans, so he observed closely. He knew the desires of the flesh, because he watched and observed the first man and woman, Adam and Eve. He saw the results of sin in their mortal bodies, their reactions to each other, their reactions to the natural things of the world, like hunger, sadness, anger, nakedness, and so forth. He observed their responses to the many challenges in their bodies.

From his observation, he now knows that God has taken on the form of flesh. He knows the needs of the flesh, the physical, spiritual, emotional needs. Just like he tempted Christ, he begins with us by saying that if we are God's children and we're hungry, we should feed ourselves (lust). Second, if we are children of God, we should throw ourselves down and make God prove Himself to us (temptation). Third, he tells us if we will bow down and worship him, then he will exalt us (idolatry).

Satan attempted to get Jesus to give in to the lust of His flesh, to tempt God to prove Himself to be who He said He was and who He said we are, and lastly, to cause Jesus to worship other gods (earthly riches). Now Jesus, being God manifested in the flesh and knowing Satan before the world began, surely could not be persuaded by Satan's worldly attempts to bring him down. Oh, yes. Jesus was God incarnate and yet flesh. Jesus, the Son of God, was not exalted to the position of King of kings and Lord of lords until He successfully defeated Satan. But it was in the flesh that Jesus defeated Satan. It was in the flesh that Jesus glorified God. Jesus was tempted as we are, yet He was without sin. We think that Jesus was without sin because He was God. No, He was without sin by choice. He willfully crucified His own flesh. Satan chose to rebel against God, an act of his free will. Jesus had the same opportunity. And more so, because unlike Satan, Jesus was subject to the dictates of the flesh nature, yet He still chose to obey God.

The Holy Ghost, Our Helper

The Holy Ghost will help us and strengthen us to do what we purpose in our heart to do. It is not that we have the ability to obey God; it is that we make the choice to. In the midst of seeing others exalted and feeling we should be in that receiving seat, in spite of wanting the God in us to perform miracles before people so they can glorify us, we deny those fleshly desires and submit our will (excruciatingly) to the purpose of God, that we may glorify God in our bodies.

Chapter 30

IN THE VOLUME OF THE BOOK
IT IS WRITTEN OF ME

I T IS IMPOSSIBLE to know Jesus without the Word and
it is impossible to know God without Jesus. Jesus said
that in the volume of the book it is written of me. It is
in the totality of the Word that we find Jesus, "and the Word
became flesh and dwelt among us." Jesus is a physical manifestation of the Word. More amazingly is the reality or the
revelation that God Himself is found in the person of Jesus
Christ. No man has ever seen God and lived. We cannot see
God, but we have seen Christ. Jesus displays every character
and attribute of God and it is done circumstantially for our
understanding. For example, God says that He will supply all
of our needs according to His riches in glory through Christ
Jesus. Jesus displays this by going to the fish's mouth and getting the money to pay taxes due and again when he takes the
three fish and five loaves and feeds the five thousand. The
provision is dispersed by God through His level or way of
provision through our Lord Jesus Christ.

So it is today, God continues to keep His promise in sup-
plying our needs. God has made promises to us through His
Son and our Lord Christ Jesus, and it is by faith in Christ
that we experience the revealed knowledge and will of God
for our lives. We have this idea of God in the cosmos somewhere up there watching over all of us taking notes and preparing to execute judgment on every mistake we make. This

God of the universe would be in direct contrast to His Son Jesus who *is* God in the flesh. Jesus said, "When you have seen me, you have seen the father." So whose report will you believe: our interpretation of God, or the God revealed in His Son Jesus?

Does God cry? Well, look at Jesus when Lazarus died. Even though Jesus knew that He could and would raise Lazarus from the dead, He still cried. Does God care about our financial needs and our physical needs? Let's look at the record, which indicates "Jesus healed all who were sick and diseased." The number of miracles our Lord performed could never be recorded since there would never be enough books to hold the recordings. Does God care about our pains, our disappointments, our emotional hurts and scars? He not only cares, but He promised to use these sufferings to produce in us joy unspeakable and full of glory.

> Beloved, think it not strange concerning the fiery trial which is to test you, as though some strange thing happened unto you, but rejoice, inasmuch as ye are partakers of Christs' sufferings, that, when His glory shall be revealed, ye may be glad also with exceeding joy.
>
> —1 PETER 4:12–13

For many of us, the idea of a supreme being who actually loves us is foreign since we have nothing to compare or understand this love to begin with. Our understanding of love is so conditional that we automatically assume that God and His love are conditional as well. Jesus never conformed, never collapsed under pressure, never lost control, and most importantly, never sinned. He was perfect, blameless, without sin, and full of love; so much love that He willingly submitted to God to be brutally tortured and murdered by His own created beings. This is how much God loves us, how much He wanted to be reconciled back to us and us to Him; this is the God of the universe, our father, and His love!

The Bible is a story about love. It is a story about a Son so committed to His Father and so full of love that He would become human to atone for His Father's creation. The centuries of pain and sorrow, the adversities and persecutions that the men and women of the Old Testament endured, were all for the purpose of preventing this loving creature from entering into the earth's sphere. The Bible is a picture of continuous years of dodging adversities and engineering circumstances all for the purpose of getting His Son here for us. If we would see the wars in the heavenlies to prevent this divine occurrence from taking place, we would be left breathless. If only we knew the height, the depth, and the breadth of the love God has for us. If only we knew what went on behind the scenes, in the spirit realm. We know the tremendous resistance in the earth, but only Revelation gives us a hint of the extent of the war in the heavenlies; all of this just for us. How much our life would change if we truly understood this love, the love that the Father has for his children.

How can we know this God of creation, this nurturing father and His love? Read the book, the Bible. It is the greatest love story ever written!

CLOSING WORDS

THANK YOU FOR taking this journey with me as I walked with my Father; my Lord and Savior Jesus the Christ; and my Best Friend, the Holy Spirit, to gain a small understanding of the height, the depth, and the width of the love that God has for us.

For God so loved the world that He gave. God had a plan from the very beginning to redeem us back to Himself. That plan included the great exchange, the sacrifice of His only begotten Son, and yet most of us do not understand the meaning of this incredible act.

God's unmerited favor is exactly as the name implies, unmerited. There is nothing that we have done, could do, or will do that would qualify us for His love. In this is love, not that we loved God, but that He loved us and gave Himself for us (1 John 4:10). God chose you, and the fact that you're reading this book is a testimony to God's desire, plan, and purpose for your life. You are not an accident, and nothing that's happened in your life to date was by chance.

We know that Christ died for our sins, we know that He rose on the third day, and we know that He is seated at the right hand of the Father, making intercession for us. But do you know that He would have done it if you were the only person on Earth? Jesus literally switched places with you. Your sin, your deserved punishment, was voluntarily taken on by Him so that you could go free. Sounds too good to be true. It is too good, and it is true. Jesus died just for you.

You may ask the question, Why me? The answer is simple:

because He loves you, and that love not only redeemed you but has a wonderful life and a wonderful future for you. God doesn't just want you to have a blessed life; He wants you to know who you really are, who He created you to be, and the potential that lies within each of us. God created us in His image and in His likeness with the ability and desire to have constant fellowship with Him. We can only know this unbelievable life *when we return to our Father.* What are you not experiencing from God because you have disqualified yourself?

God had *you* in mind when He ordained this book. I look forward to hearing from you as to how this book has blessed and transformed your life.

—BEVERLY D. THOMAS

ABOUT THE AUTHOR

BEVERLY D. THOMAS was born and raised in South Central Los Angeles. She is the second of six children born to a young mother who turned fifteen just one month before Beverly's birth and a nineteen-year-old father who she would meet for the first time at age fourteen. Growing up in a dysfunctional environment and experiencing years of physical and sexual abuse is where Beverly credits her determination to succeed and provide a better life for herself and her family. Although she was introduced to Jesus Christ at the age of sixteen, as a result of the pain, anger, and inability to attach, it would be decades later before this introduction would transform itself into a personal and intimate relationship with God through Christ and His precious Holy Spirit.

Today, she lives a life passionate about her Lord and shares His love to all who are blessed to grace her path. Beverly is a proud mother of three beautiful children and a grandmother of three incredible grandchildren. Beverly holds a Bachelor of Science Degree in Human Services and a Master of Science Degree in Counseling Psychology. As a Marriage and Family Therapist, she has the privilege of counseling and ministering to individuals who are experiencing some of the same trauma that she experienced growing up.

Beverly is a much sought-after speaker for her work as an advocate for at-risk youth. A former foster child and foster parent, she is able to minister and teach from a perspective that is life changing. Beverly serves on a number of committees and boards that service the community.

CONTACT THE AUTHOR

WEBSITE:

BEVERLYTHOMAS.COM

E-MAIL:

BEBBES118@GMAIL.COM